P9-EMQ-799

DEADLY DISEASES AND EPIDEMICS

DIPHTHERIA

DEADLY DISEASES AND EPIDEMICS

Anthrax, Second Edition
Antibiotic-Resistant Bacteria
Avian Flu
Botulisim
Campylobacteriosis
Cervical Cancer
Chicken Pox
Cholera, Second Edition
Dengue Fever and Other Hemorrhagic Viruses
Diphtheria
Ebola
Encephalitis
Escherichia coli Infections
Gonorrhea
Hantavirus Pulmonary Syndrome
Helicobacter pylori
Hepatitis
Herpes
HIV/AIDS
Infectious Diseases of the Mouth
Infectious Fungi
Influenza, Second Edition
Legionnaires' Disease
Leprosy
Lung Cancer
Lyme Disease
Mad Cow Disease
Malaria, Second Edition
Meningitis
Mononucleosis, Second Edition
Pelvic Inflammatory Disease
Plague, Second Edition
Polio, Second Edition
Prostate Cancer
Rabies
Rocky Mountain Spotted Fever
Rubella and Rubeola
Salmonella
SARS, Second Edition
Smallpox
Staphylococcus aureus Infections
Streptococcus (Group A)
Streptococcus (Group B)
Syphilis, Second Edition
Tetanus
Toxic Shock Syndrome
Trypanosomiasis
Tuberculosis
Tularemia
Typhoid Fever
West Nile Virus
Yellow Fever

DEADLY DISEASES AND EPIDEMICS

DIPHTHERIA

Patrick Guilfoile, Ph.D.

CONSULTING EDITOR
Hilary Babcock, M.D., M.P.H.,
Infectious Diseases Division,
Washington University School of Medicine,
Medical Director of Occupational Health (Infectious Diseases),
Barnes-Jewish Hospital and St. Louis Children's Hospital

FOREWORD BY
David Heymann
World Health Organization

Deadly Diseases and Epidemics: Diphtheria

Chelsea House
An imprint of Infobase Publishing
132 West 31st Street
New York, NY 10001

Library of Congress Cataloging-in-Publication Data
Guilfoile, Patrick.
Diphtheria / Patrick Guilfoile ; consulting editor, Hilary Babcock ; foreword by David Heymann.
p. cm. — (Deadly diseases and epidemics)
Includes bibliographical references and index.
ISBN-13: 978-1-60413-228-1 (alk. paper)
ISBN-10: 1-60413-228-0 (alk. paper)
1. Diphtheria—Popular works. I. Title.
RC138.G85 2009
616.9'313—dc22
2008038965

Chelsea House books are available at special discounts when purchased in bulk quantities for businesses, associations, institutions, or sales promotions. Please call our Special Sales Department in New York at (212) 967-8800 or (800) 322-8755.

You can find Chelsea House on the World Wide Web at http://www.chelseahouse.com

Series design by Terry Mallon
Cover design by Keith Trego

Printed in the United States of America

Bang EJB 10 9 8 7 6 5 4 3 2 1

This book is printed on acid-free paper.

All links and Web addresses were checked and verified to be correct at the time of publication. Because of the dynamic nature of the Web, some addresses and links may have changed since publication and may no longer be valid.

Table of Contents

Foreword

Communicable diseases kill and cause long-term disability. The microbial agents that cause them are dynamic, changeable, and resilient: They are responsible for more than 14 million deaths each year, mainly in developing countries.

Approximately 46 percent of all deaths in the developing world are due to communicable diseases, and almost 90 percent of these deaths are from AIDS, tuberculosis, malaria, and acute diarrheal and respiratory infections of children. In addition to causing great human suffering, these high-mortality communicable diseases have become major obstacles to economic development. They are a challenge to control either because of the lack of effective vaccines, or because the drugs that are used to treat them are becoming less effective because of antimicrobial drug resistance.

Millions of people, especially those who are poor and living in developing countries, are also at risk from disabling communicable diseases such as polio, leprosy, lymphatic filariasis, and onchocerciasis. In addition to human suffering and permanent disability, these communicable diseases create an economic burden—both on the workforce that handicapped persons are unable to join, and on their families and society, upon which they must often depend for economic support.

Finally, the entire world is at risk of the unexpected communicable diseases, those that are called emerging or re-emerging infections. Infection is often unpredictable because risk factors for transmission are not understood, or because it often results from organisms that cross the species barrier from animals to humans. The cause is often viral, such as Ebola and Marburg hemorrhagic fevers and severe acute respiratory syndrome (SARS). In addition to causing human suffering and death, these infections place health workers at great risk and are costly to economies. Infections such as Bovine Spongiform Encephalopathy (BSE) and the associated new human variant of Creutzfeldt-Jakob Disease (vCJD) in Europe, and avian influenza A (H5N1) in Asia, are reminders of the seriousness of emerging and re-emerging infections. In addition, many of these infections have the potential to cause pandemics, which are a constant threat to our economies and public health security.

Science has given us vaccines and anti-infective drugs that have helped keep infectious diseases under control. Nothing demonstrates the effectiveness of vaccines better than the successful eradication of smallpox, the decrease in polio as the eradication program continues, and the decrease in measles when routine immunization programs are supplemented by mass vaccination campaigns.

Likewise, the effectiveness of anti-infective drugs is clearly demonstrated through prolonged life or better health in those infected with viral diseases such as AIDS, parasitic infections such as malaria, and bacterial infections such as tuberculosis and pneumococcal pneumonia.

But current research and development is not filling the pipeline for new anti-infective drugs as rapidly as resistance is developing, nor is vaccine development providing vaccines for some of the most common and lethal communicable diseases. At the same time providing people with access to existing anti-infective drugs, vaccines, and goods such as condoms or bed nets—necessary for the control of communicable diseases in many developing countries—remains a great challenge.

Education, experimentation, and the discoveries that grow from them, are the tools needed to combat high mortality infectious diseases, diseases that cause disability, or emerging and re-emerging infectious diseases. At the same time, partnerships between developing and industrialized countries can overcome many of the challenges of access to goods and technologies. This book may inspire its readers to set out on the path of drug and vaccine development, or on the path to discovering better public health technologies by applying our present understanding of the human genome and those of various infectious agents. Readers may likewise be inspired to help ensure wider access to those protective goods and technologies. Such inspiration, with pragmatic action, will keep us on the winning side of the struggle against communicable diseases.

David L. Heymann
Assistant Director General,
Health Security and Environment
Representative of the Director General for Polio Eradication
World Health Organization
Geneva, Switzerland

Acknowledgements

Thanks to my wife, Audrey, for her support of this project and for her talented assistance in helping prepare several figures for the book. I also thank my father, Thomas Guilfoile, for his expert proofreading assistance and editing suggestions. Of course any errors or omissions that I've made are my responsibility alone. I appreciate the assistance I received from the interlibrary loan staff at the A.C. Clark Library, Pat Connelly, and Robin Schulte, who facilitated my getting a number of old and obscure references. I also appreciate the encouragement I received for doing this work from my colleagues, Dr. Joann Fredrickson and Carol Nielsen.

1

What Is Diphtheria?

In 2003, a 63-year-old man from Pennsylvania traveled to Haiti to help build a church. It was a weeklong trip, and he developed a sore throat the day before he returned home. Two days after the trip ended, he went to the emergency room complaining of a severe sore throat and difficulty swallowing, and he was given an antibiotic. He returned to the hospital the next day with more serious symptoms, including difficulty breathing, and was admitted to the intensive care unit. During the process of inserting a tube down his throat to assist with his breathing, growths were noted, suggesting diphtheria. He was given multiple antibiotics, diphtheria antitoxin, and steroids. His condition continued to deteriorate, and 17 days after he developed symptoms, he died of heart failure. Further laboratory tests confirmed diphtheria. This patient had never been vaccinated, and even though he was given intensive medical care, his body succumbed to the effects of the toxin produced by this microbe.[1]

Diphtheria is an acute respiratory disease caused by the bacterium *Corynebacterium diphtheriae*. The symptoms of the disease are primarily the result of a powerful toxin produced by the bacteria. In the United States in 1900, diphtheria was the tenth leading cause of death. Today, because of advances in medical science, in a typical year no one dies of diphtheria in the United States.

Immunity to diphtheria can develop either from natural exposure to the organism or from vaccination. In either case, repeated exposures to the organism (or the material in the vaccine) are required to develop and maintain immunity. Widespread vaccination against diphtheria started in the 1940s, and the disease became rare in the developed world within a couple of decades. A major vaccine initiative began in developing countries in the 1970s, and the number of cases of diphtheria has dropped in those countries as well. Since 2000, there have been fewer than 15,000 cases worldwide, per year. The microbe that causes diphtheria is still widely distributed around the globe. When medical care deteriorates and/or the rate of vaccination declines, the disease can make a comeback, as it has in several parts of the world in recent years.[2] Diphtheria remains a serious disease wherever it occurs: Even with the most advanced medical treatment, 5 to 10 percent of patients who develop a severe case of diphtheria die.

CHARACTERISTICS OF THE ORGANISM

C. diphtheriae is a **gram-positive**, rod-shaped bacterium. The Gram's stain is used to distinguish two broad groups of bacteria: gram positive and gram negative. Gram-positive bacteria stain purple when treated with a series of stains and decolorizing agents. Gram-positive bacteria have a thick cell wall and a single cell membrane. *Corynebacteria* have a club-shaped appearance, which accounts for the genus name (*coryne* means "club" in Greek). When isolated from the throat or collected from certain types of laboratory media, *C. diphtheriae* cells often

ORIGIN OF THE TERM "DIPHTHERIA"

The French physician Pierre Bretonneau performed autopsies on many people who had died of what we now call diphtheria. He noted that a common feature of these victims was that they all had a growth, called a pseudomembrane, in their upper respiratory tract. In 1826, he first used the term "diphtherite," after the Greek word meaning "leather or hide," based on the leather-like appearance of the pseudomembrane. The term was subsequently modified to "diphtheria" in the 1850s.[3]

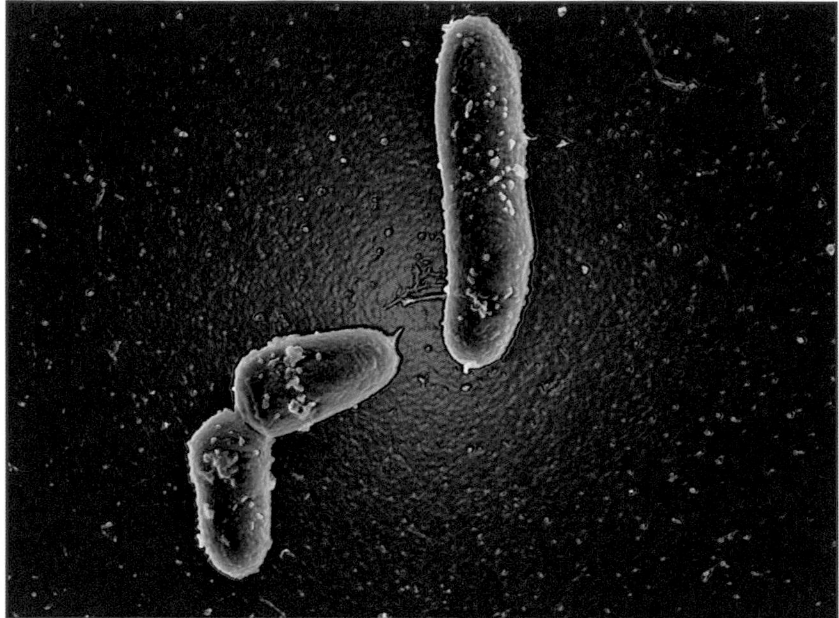

Figure 1.1 The *Corynebacterium diphtheriae*, shown here, is the bacterium that causes diphtheria. (© Mediscan/Visuals Unlimited, Inc.)

have the appearance of a picket fence when viewed through the microscope. This is a consequence of an unusual form of cell division, called "snapping." Following cell division, one of the cells of the newly divided pair folds back toward the other recently divided cell.[4]

C. diphtheriae is primarily found in the upper respiratory tract of infected people, although it occasionally causes skin infections. There are four subspecies or **biotypes** of *C. diphtheriae*. These biotypes can be distinguished in several ways, including the size of their colonies on solid laboratory medium, the characteristics of their growth in liquid medium, their ability or inability to ferment starch, and the severity of disease they cause.[5]

One biotype, *C. diphtheriae gravis*, tends to cause the most severe diphtheria infections. The other biotypes, *C. diphtheriae intermedius*, *C. diphtheriae belfanti*, and *C. diphtheriae mitus*, typically cause less severe forms of the disease. Since the symptoms of diphtheria are almost entirely caused by the toxin, the severity of disease normally corresponds with the amount of toxin a strain produces. Not surprisingly, *gravis* strains tend to have higher levels of toxin production, compared to the other biotypes.

DISEASES CAUSED BY *CORYNEBACTERIUM DIPHTHERIAE*

In addition to the respiratory form of diphtheria, *C. diphtheriae* can cause skin rashes or skin ulcers. Typically, the organism infects a preexisting wound. An ulcer is the most common type of skin infection caused by this microbe. Initially, infection may occur at the site of a prior, often minor, trauma causing redness and pain, until the lesion eventually opens. Within a short period of time, a gaping sore develops that can be an inch or more across. These wounds are painful for a couple of weeks or so, and may be covered by a gray or brown pseudomembrane. Once the membrane falls off, the wound becomes a red, open, oozing sore. The surrounding tissue is discolored and often filled with fluid.[6,7] Although an unpleasant and potentially long-lasting infection, this form of the disease is generally relatively mild and can be easily treated. However, skin infections may lead to transmission of diphtheria to the respiratory tract of nonimmune individuals.

Skin infections with *C. diphtheriae* are relatively rare in economically privileged regions of the world. In these areas, this form of diphtheria has been most commonly reported in homeless people; no more than a handful of cases per year probably occur in the United States currently. In contrast, skin infections with this microbe are fairly common in some tropical regions, and this exposure to *C. diphtheriae* may result in high levels of natural immunity to respiratory infection with this microbe in those areas. Apparently enough toxin enters the tissues from the wound to lead to an immune response, although the toxin levels are typically not high enough to cause serious damage and disease. This may explain why diphtheria outbreaks have typically occurred in temperate regions, where these types of skin infections are rare and therefore levels of natural immunity, at least in children, are lower.

Diphtheria can also cause infections anywhere along the respiratory system. *C. diphtheriae*, at least in temperate areas, is typically associated with respiratory infections. These infections can occur in any respiratory tissues, such as the nose, but are most often found in the throat.

Nasal diphtheria initially shows the same symptoms as the common cold, with a runny nose being the first indication of illness. Eventually, a membrane forms on the tissue between the nostrils, and the nasal mucus may be colored with blood. Apparently the toxin produced by *C. diphtheriae* is not readily absorbed into the body from nasal passages. Consequently, nasal diphtheria is typically not life threatening and can be easily treated with **antibiotics.**[8] Antibiotics are drugs that kill bacteria without harming the person who is infected. While not seriously ill themselves, patients with nasal diphtheria can easily spread infection to others.

In contrast with nasal diphtheria, respiratory diphtheria is a very serious disease. Prior to the development of effective medical treatments, about half the people who developed symptoms of respiratory diphtheria died. In children who have diphtheria, the bacteria grow primarily in the upper and lower throat. *C. diphtheriae* attaches to the surface of respiratory tissues and produces toxin. As noted previously, the toxin is primarily responsible for the symptoms of the disease. Transmission of respiratory diphtheria is through close contact with an infected person. This can occur through direct contact with the nasal or respiratory secretions from an infected person.

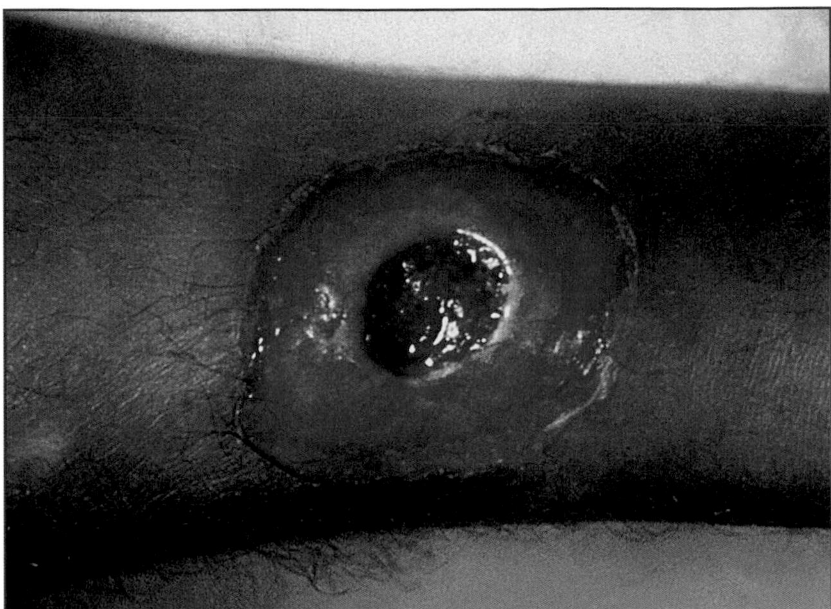

Figure 1.2 Diphtheria skin infections cause oozing sores, but in general are less severe and more treatable than respiratory diphtheria. This is a diphtheria lesion on a leg. (CDC/Dr. Brodsky)

It can also occur through inhalation of organisms that have become airborne through a patient coughing or sneezing. In outbreaks since 1980, which have occurred primarily in adults, infection is commonly found in the mouth, with other sites of infection including the cheeks, tongue, and lips.

SYMPTOMS AND OTHER CHARACTERISTICS OF THE DISEASE

Unlike many bacterial pathogens that work their way inside the body, *C. diphtheriae* remains on or near the surface of the tissues. From that location, the organism releases its toxin. As a consequence, the surrounding tissue dies and a flap of tissue (a pseudomembrane) begins to form as a result

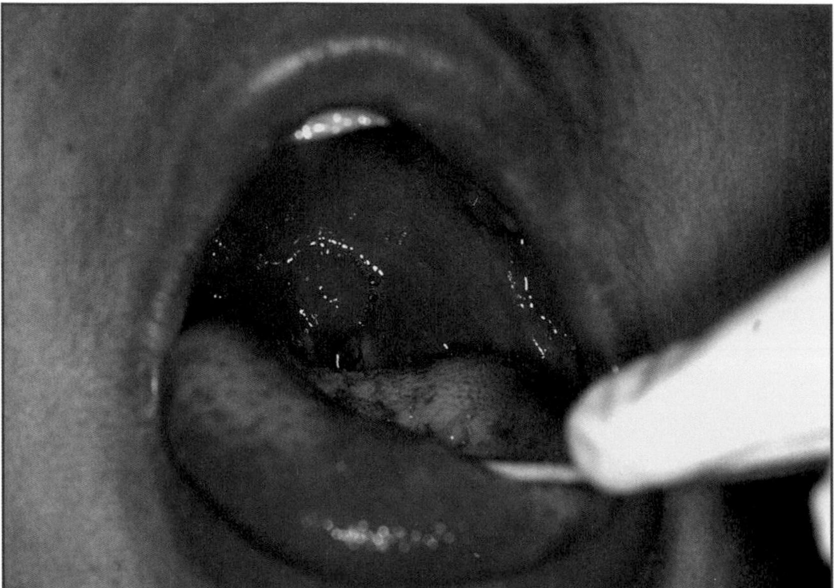

Figure 1.3 Diphtheria causes a pseudomembrane to grow at the back of the throat. This growth, shown above, can block the respiratory tract. (© Gary Gaugler/Visuals Unlimited, Inc.)

of tissue destruction, deposition of a protein called fibrin, and accumulation of bacteria and the remains of dead cells from the throat. If the pseudomembrane becomes extensive enough, it can block the respiratory tract, causing death by suffocation. Initially the pseudomembrane is white or yellow, typically taking on a more gray hue as the infection proceeds. At later stages of the disease, tissue death in the membrane often results in black or green patches, and a very strong, unpleasant odor. Often, additional sites of infection and pseudomembrane formation occur in the lower respiratory and digestive tracts.

Symptoms of diphtheria typically develop two to five days after infection, though the incubation period can sometimes be as long as 10 days. In early stages, this obstruction of the respiratory tract causes hoarseness, coughing, and breathing difficulty. As noted above, the formation of a pseudomembrane in the respiratory tract is a key feature of the disease. The **lymph nodes** around the neck often become swollen. Lymph nodes are an element of the immune system that filter out pathogens. Lymph nodes become swollen when trying to respond to infection with a pathogen. In severe cases, this swelling becomes pronounced, leading to a thickening of the neck called "bull neck." Normally, a fever is present, but it is generally below 103°F. In addition, patients typically have a sore throat, headache, and weakness. At more advanced stages, the skin of patients may be tinged blue, which is an indication of a lack of oxygen reaching the lungs due to the constriction of the respiratory passages.

With modern medical treatment, death from suffocation occurring as a result of the pseudomembrane blocking the respiratory tract is rare. In the developed world, most fatal cases of diphtheria are the result of the toxin spreading throughout the body and damaging the heart, causing heart failure. This type of damage is more likely to occur in patients who have a more severe case of diphtheria. A substantial number of patients with heart damage caused by diphtheria toxin never recover completely and end up with some type of permanent cardiac impairment.

Paralysis or other nerve damage can also occur as a result of the action of the toxin on the nerves and muscles, and this has been reported in about 10 percent of symptomatic infections with *C. diphtheriae*. The more serious the initial symptoms of diphtheria, the more likely the patient will experience nerve damage. One common, early site of nerve damage is the soft palate. This results in paralysis of the soft palate and throat. When this occurs, fluids taken in through the mouth are passed back up through the nose, rather than being swallowed. This initial sign of nerve damage is

(continues on page 20)

DIPHTHERIA AND THE IDITAROD

Nome is a small town in northwest Alaska, located on the Bering Sea, just a short distance south of the Arctic Circle. It is a very remote place and, even today, no roads or railroads link Nome to the outside world. Back in the 1920s, once the ice closed in each winter and ships could no longer reach the town, there was no contact with the outside world for seven months except via telegraph and dogsled. When the last ship left in the fall of 1925, the town's doctor, Dr. Curtis Welch, made a realization—the diphtheria antitoxin that he had ordered did not arrive. (Antitoxins are medicines that interact with toxins and prevent the toxins from functioning. More specifically, antitoxins contain antibodies, which bind to the toxin.) That meant he had only a small supply of expired diphtheria antitoxin, but he was not too worried, as he had not seen a case of diphtheria in Nome in the 18 years he had been the town's physician.

However, by December, Dr. Welch had noticed that an unusual number of children had developed sore throats and tonsillitis. Around Christmas, he started becoming concerned that some of the cases of tonsillitis might actually be diphtheria. By January 20, a child showed clear symptoms of diphtheria, and two days later, Dr. Welch sent a request to the U.S. Public Health Service for a supply of diphtheria antitoxin.

Some antitoxin was available from other towns in Alaska, and this was quickly put on a northbound train from Anchorage. The problem was how to get the antitoxin from the train stop to Nome, a distance of about 700 miles. Two options were considered. Commercial aviation was just developing in Alaska, and promoters of this new mode of transportation clamored to transport antitoxin to Nome by plane. However, a combination of cold temperatures and outdated planes, suitable only for summer transport, made this option unworkable.

That left dogsled teams as the only option for transporting the antitoxin. The antitoxin was brought by train from Anchorage to Neena. Once the train arrived at the town of Neena, after a journey of about 24 hours, the antitoxin was transferred to the first dogsled team. From there, the precious cargo was transported over difficult and hazardous terrain 674 miles to Nome. This took about five-and-a-half days and required a total of 20 different dog teams. Along the route, the air temperature was below -60°F in places. Consequently, several of the mushers and their dogs suffered from frostbite, but the serum arrived in good condition and was used to treat a number of ill patients. All together, at least 70 residents of Nome developed diphtheria, and at least six died from the disease. Before the availability of antitoxin, the death rate from diphtheria approached 50 percent, so the antitoxin may have prevented upward of 30 deaths. The bravery of the dogs and the mushers was celebrated, and one dog in particular, Balto, became commemorated in film and books, although other sled dogs had also played an important role in the safe delivery of the antitoxin.

In 1967, a 25-mile dog sled race was held to celebrate America's purchase of Alaska and to honor the memory of one of the mushers who helped transport the antitoxin to Nome, Leonhard Seppala. The first race to go the entire distance from Anchorage to Nome was held in 1973, and it was called the Iditarod (the name of the trail used for the race). Although it does not entirely follow the same route as the antitoxin run in 1925, the Iditarod race is widely considered, in part, to commemorate the brave dogsled teams that delivered lifesaving medicine to the residents of Nome.

(continued from page 17)

sometimes followed by more general nerve impairment, which may take place as long as three months after the initial symptoms of diphtheria appear. The degree of impairment can be quite variable, with some patients experiencing minor muscle weakness and some experiencing total paralysis. Typically, patients recover from these symptoms without permanent damage, although recovery may take a long time.

TRANSMISSION OF DIPHTHERIA

Diphtheria is usually transmitted by contact with an infected person's respiratory secretions, for example, when the person sneezes or coughs. However, there have been apparent cases of transmission from articles that have been contaminated by a person with diphtheria, and the organism has been found on the pillows or bedsheets of patients with diphtheria.[9] There has also been a report from Yemen of diphtheria transmission from milk or milk products containing this microbe.[10] Transmission of diphtheria can also occur from a skin infection to the respiratory tract of a susceptible person. The risk of transmission is considered greatest among people who have been in close contact with the infected person, including members of the same household and school classmates who share a classroom or a dormitory.

DIPHTHERIA IN OTHER ANIMALS

Generally, it is thought that *C. diphtheriae* infects only humans, but there have been a few reports of *C. diphtheriae* infection in other animals. For example, a horse was reported to have diphtheria based on a report by a medical health officer in 1908.[11] However, based on epidemiological data, it is clear that all or almost all transmission of diphtheria is person-to-person and that animals are not likely a major source of this disease.

Another bacterium, *C. ulcerans*, does infect animals and can cause diphtheria-like disease in humans. In addition, there is the potential for this microbe to transfer its DNA to

C. diphtheriae, which could raise concerns about transmission of toxin genes and other **virulence factors** between the two organisms. This could also limit the potential to eliminate diphtheria entirely, as a strain of *C. diphtheria* lacking the toxin gene could theoretically regain the ability to produce toxin by acquiring the gene from *C. ulcerans*.

RELATED ORGANISMS

A number of bacteria are closely related to *C. diphtheriae* and can also cause disease in humans (Table 1.1). These include *C. amycolatum*, which causes skin infections; *C. jeikeium*, which causes urinary tract infections and infections of the heart; *C. striatum*, which can cause respiratory infections; *C. pseudodiphtheriticum*, which can cause infections of the heart; and *C. urealyticum*, which can cause urinary tract infections. In most cases, these diseases primarily affect people who have some underlying medical condition that makes them more susceptible to infection.[12] Another important pathogen is

Table 1.1 Diseases Caused by Some *Corynebacterium* Species

Organism	Diseases
C. diphtheriae	respiratory diphtheria, skin infections
C. ulcerans	skin infections, respiratory diphtheria
C. amycolatum	skin infections
C. jeikeium	urinary tract infections, heart infections
C. striatum	respiratory infections
C. pseudodiphtheriticum	heart infections
C. urealyticum	urinary tract infections

C. ulcerans, which has been identified as a cause of skin ulcers. Some strains of *C. ulcerans* can produce the same toxin found in *C. diphtheriae*.[13] A better understanding of these related microbes should provide additional clues to help clarify why *C. diphtheriae* has been such a successful pathogen.

2

History of Diphtheria

The Woman, who suffered from sore throat ... started just with her voice becoming indistinct. Her tongue was red and parched.

***First Day**: shivering, high fever.*

***Third Day**: rigor, high fever, a hard reddish swelling on either side of the neck down to the chest, extremities cold and livid: respiration superficial. What she drank was regurgitated through the nostrils and she was unable to swallow. Stools and urine suppressed.*

***Fourth Day**: All symptoms more pronounced.*

***Fifth Day**: Dies.*[1]

There are varying interpretations of whether the disease described by Hippocrates in the seventh century B.C. was actually the earliest description of diphtheria, though it does describe some symptoms accurately. For example, diphtheria frequently causes paralysis of the palate, causing liquids to be expelled through the nose. A second century A.D. account by Aretaeus of Cappadocia gave a more generally accepted description of a disease that is consistent with diphtheria:

> The manner of death is most piteous; pain sharp and hot as from carbuncle; respiration bad, for their breath smells strongly of putrefaction, as they constantly inhale the same again into their chest; they are in so loathsome a state that they cannot endure the smell of themselves ... Hoarseness, loss of speech supervene; and these symptoms hurry on from bad to worse, until suddenly, falling to the ground, they expire.[2]

OTHER HISTORICAL ACCOUNTS OF DIPHTHERIA

Caelius Aurelianus, who lived during the third century A.D., described breathing difficulty, a barking voice, and a reddened face as symptoms of a serious disease. He also described how some afflicted individuals expelled fluids through their nose when attempting to swallow, a common manifestation of a paralysis of the soft palate that frequently accompanies severe cases of diphtheria. There is also reference to a disease called Askara (which translates to "stop up" or "choke") in the Talmud, the rabbinic writings that date to around the fifth century A.D., which scholars have interpreted as describing epidemic diphtheria. In the sixth century A.D., Aetius of Amida described a disease that resulted in spots on the pharynx, which often became raw.[3] Thereafter, the disease disappeared from the historical record for nearly 1,000 years. It is likely that diphtheria remained a killer; the limited written documentation from this period probably explains its "disappearance."

The next reports of diphtheria were from Holland in 1557. Within decades, the disease became widespread in Europe. For example, in Spain, outbreaks occurred every 20 to 40 years, starting in 1583. The disease there was called *morbus suffocans* ("the suffocating illness") or *El garatillo* ("the strangler"). The symptoms of the disease that were reported included a sore throat and the presence of a membrane in the upper respiratory tract. Based on records from more recent epidemics, upward of 50 percent of the severely affected patients probably succumbed to diphtheria.

DIPHTHERIA OUTBREAKS PRIOR TO THE AVAILABILITY OF EFFECTIVE TREATMENT

Periodic diphtheria outbreaks continued into the nineteenth century, both in Europe and the United States. Little information is available regarding diphtheria outside of North America and Europe during this period, although it is likely that diphtheria was widely distributed over much of the world.

A particularly deadly outbreak of diphtheria started in 1857 in the United States and Europe, and it continued until about 1900. Yearly mortality rates were as high as 1 per 1,000 per year, and sometimes even higher.[4] For example, in Philadelphia, Pennsylvania, between 1860 and 1864, there were 1,925 deaths due to diphtheria (1,803 of those deaths were of children 15 and under). The population of Philadelphia was 565,529 in 1860, so the death rate from diphtheria was about 3 deaths per 1,000 people over that five-year period (and much higher among children). In New York City, a total of 875 deaths in 1860 and 1861 were caused by diphtheria. With a population of 813,669 in 1860, that would translate to a death rate, during that two-year period, of about 1 death per 1,000.[5]

IDEAS ABOUT THE CAUSE OF DIPHTHERIA DURING THE 1800s

Well into the late 1800s, physicians had no real understanding of the cause of diphtheria (or other diseases). For example, explanations proposed for diphtheria in the nineteenth century included some agent of the occult, a poisonous atmosphere (often air associated with swamps or marshes), or gases given off by decaying animals. There was also an association made with diphtheria and damp, cold weather, and living in low-lying areas.

Fortunately, the idea that many diseases are caused by specific microbes was developed during the 1870s. This concept led to the discovery of the bacterium that causes anthrax in 1876. The discovery a few years later of a specific bacterium that causes diphtheria helped pave the way for a true understanding of the disease, improved methods of diagnosis, and ultimately, allowed for the development of an effective means of treatment and prevention.

In 1883, Edwin Klebs, a microbiologist working in Germany, reported that he had identified two types of bacteria in pseudomembranes removed from patients who had diphtheria.

One type of bacteria formed chains of round ball-shaped bacteria; the other was a rod-shaped bacterium. His research convinced him that the rod-shaped bacteria were responsible for the disease. However, he was not able to isolate this microbe from all other bacteria, so he was unable to establish with certainty that this bacterium was, indeed, the cause of diphtheria.[6]

ISOLATING THE BACTERIUM THAT CAUSES DIPHTHERIA

Shortly after the studies conducted by Edwin Klebs were published, Fredrick Loeffler, another German microbiologist, reported a series of experiments in 1884 that ultimately led to the isolation and characterization of the bacterium that causes diphtheria. His work was pivotal for the subsequent development of methods for treating and preventing diphtheria.

Loeffler first developed an improved method of staining bacteria so they could be more readily visualized in the tissues of patients with disease. His staining technique involved the use of methylene blue dye, which was dissolved in alcohol and treated with potassium hydroxide to produce a basic solution. The bacteria present in the tissues stained much more intensely when exposed to this stain, compared to the human cells surrounding them.[7] He then examined tissue from 27 patients with diphtheria. Using his staining method, he, like Klebs, determined that there were two candidate bacteria that could be responsible for the disease. One type formed chains of small, ball-like bacteria and were located on the surface of tissues in the throat, including the surface of the pseudomembrane. A second possible microbe was "the Klebs bacterium," a somewhat irregular, rod-shaped microbe previously described by Klebs that was primarily found just below the surface of the pseudomembrane.

The next step in identifying the pathogen was to try to grow the two types of bacteria in pure laboratory culture. For

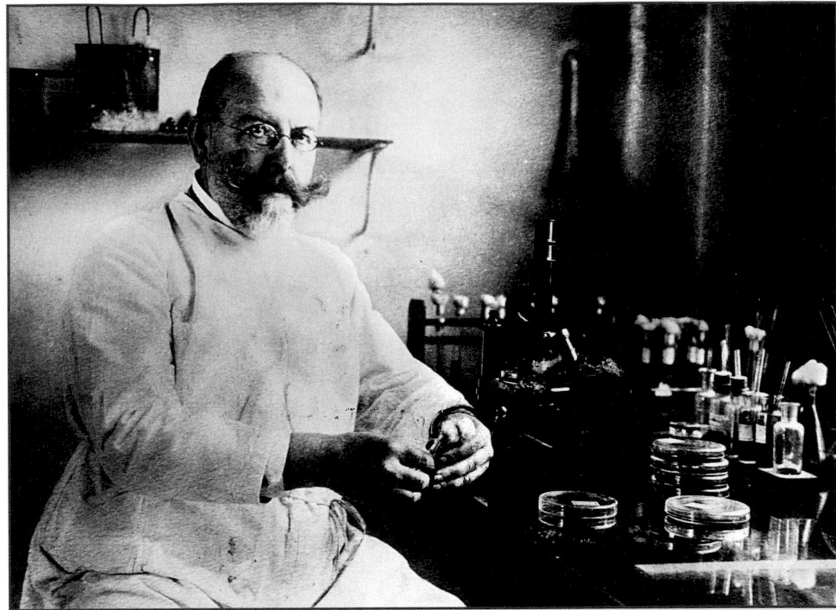

Figure 2.1 Fredrick Loeffler, a German microbiologist, developed methods of isolating *C. diphtheriae* and differentiating between this bacterium and other bacterial specimens. (© Bettmann/CORBIS)

the ball-like bacterium, fragments of infected tonsils from patients were put into a meat broth-gelatin medium. The isolated colonies that developed in this medium presumably arose from single bacteria, so the colonies represented a pure, single type of microbe. Bacteria from the isolated colonies were then put into new meat broth-gelatin medium cultures sequentially two more times to assure that they were indeed **pure cultures.** A pure culture consists of just a single type of organism.

Next, the ball-shaped bacterium was tested to determine if this microbe could cause a similar disease in an animal. Loeffler used four separate pure cultures of this microbe in animal experiments; he attempted to infect birds, mice, guinea pigs, rabbits, dogs, and apes with this organism. Loeffler was not able to observe symptoms of diphtheria-like disease in any of the animals tested; consequently, he felt it was not likely this microbe that was the cause of diphtheria. In fact, the organism he isolated was likely a member of the genus *Streptococcus*, a group that includes *Streptococcus pyogenes*, a microbe that causes a serious type of sore throat, which is frequently referred to as strep throat. *Streptococcal* species are common inhabitants of the throat, even in healthy people.

Loeffler then proceeded to take similar steps to determine if the Klebs bacterium was indeed the cause of diphtheria. An initial stumbling block was the fact that this microbe would not grow on the same medium that allowed growth of the ball-like bacterium. Consequently, he instead used coagulated sheep blood containing 25 percent broth as a growth substrate for this organism.

For this stage of his research, he used throat scrapings from a patient who had died of diphtheria. He put the throat scrapings on the coagulated sheep's blood broth. After one day, colonies of the rod-shaped bacteria had grown up on the surface of the blood clot. These colonies were then transferred to new preparations of coagulated sheep blood-broth medium. After one more passage in sheep blood broth, the cultures were considered pure and were ready to be used for animal experiments. Altogether, he used six different pure cultures of this bacterium in animal experiments.

Loeffler tested a wide variety of animals to determine if any would show diphtheria-like symptoms when exposed to the Klebs bacterium. He found that mice, rats, and the "long-tailed Java ape" showed no signs of illness when exposed to this bacterium. A number of other animals (guinea pigs, canaries, pigeons, chickens, and rabbits) did show disease symptoms when inoculated with this microbe. In particular, when the Klebs bacterium was injected into guinea pigs, the animals rapidly became listless and their fur disheveled; typically, they died within a week. At the site of injection, a membrane formed, analogous to the pseudomembrane that forms in human patients. Similarly, when pigeons were exposed to this microbe through a **tracheotomy** (a surgical method for creating an opening in the throat), they developed a pseudomembrane in that location, providing further confirmation of the connection between diphtheria and the Klebs bacterium, now known as *C. diphtheriae.*

At this point, Loeffler now had a good **assay** for the presence of *C. diphtheriae.* (An assay, in this context, means a procedure for detecting a microbe.) He could grow the bacterium on the surface of coagulated blood, then inject the purified microbe into guinea pigs and look for symptoms associated with diphtheria. With this assay in hand, he decided to pursue the question of whether or not one could find the diphtheria bacterium in healthy individuals. He swabbed the throats of 20 children, and plated the samples on an appropriate microbiological medium. One of the 20 cultures contained a bacterium that looked like *C. diphtheriae.* When this bacterium was injected into guinea pigs, the animals died after showing the same symptoms as guinea pigs that were injected with *C. diphtheriae,* suggesting this microbe was indeed *C. diphtheriae.*

This result, difficult to interpret at the time, suggested that this pathogenic microbe did not, under some conditions, cause disease in humans. This puzzling observation did not have a complete explanation for decades, but it ultimately would be important for understanding the transmission of diphtheria from person to person. Unfortunately for Loeffler, this observation did leave some room for doubt about this organism being the cause of diphtheria, since a bacterium normally thought to be pathogenic was found in a healthy person without disease. At this point, Loeffler resorted to describing hunches he had about what factors might contribute to susceptibility to diphtheria, and, therefore, an explanation for this finding of a healthy person who harbored the pathogen. For example (in company with generations of grandmothers), he pointed to what are now generally considered unfounded concerns about the weather, specifically the "effect of sharp north or northeast winds" on enhancing susceptibility to infection. But he also did provide evidence of the development of immunity to diphtheria in guinea pigs, and his argument that humans could also become immune eventually became accepted and ultimately provided an explanation for the presence of *C. diphtheriae* in the throats of individuals who were not ill.[8]

Loeffler's work opened a number of important avenues for further investigation. For example, one of the observations he had made in his guinea pig experiments was that, when the animals were examined following death, bacteria were found only at the site of injection. However, the damage to the tissues and organs was found throughout the body of the animal, suggesting the action of a toxin that is produced by the microbes and travels via the circulatory system. This was a critical observation, since it quickly became clear that the toxin was the primary factor that caused the symptoms of diphtheria. Loeffler initially followed up on this observation himself and attempted to extract the diphtheria toxin from bacterial cultures. For example, he reported on experiments where he grew *C. diphtheriae* in a solution containing sterile, minced pieces of beef. After four or five days, he added glycerol to the cultures and used alcohol to make the proteins (including, he hoped, the toxin) come out of solution. The solid material was filtered out, dried, and resuspended in water. This material was treated again with alcohol, this time in the presence of carbon dioxide, filtered, dried, and then resuspended in water. When a substantial amount of this material (0.1 to 0.2 grams) was injected into guinea pigs, it produced an initial violent, painful reaction and longer-term effects, similar to the injection of *C. diphtheriae* bacteria. This suggested that the toxin was present in Loeffler's preparations, but it was not very potent and not very pure. Consequently, he was limited in his ability to further study the toxin.

ISOLATION OF THE DIPHTHERIA TOXIN

At about the same time, two colleagues at the Pasteur Institute in France were also working on purifying the diphtheria toxin. In a paper published in 1888, Emile Roux and Alexander Yersin confirmed the work of Loeffler that suggested that *C. diphtheriae* does not spread throughout the body, but rather does its damage while remaining localized at the site of infection.

In their experiments to isolate diphtheria toxin, Roux and Yersin grew *C. diphtheriae* for seven days in a broth medium. This length of incubation was one reason their experiments were more successful than Loeffler's—who incubated the bacteria for four to five days—since toxin tends to accumulate to higher levels in older cultures. This culture was poured through a porcelain filter to separate the bacteria from the liquid. After verifying that the liquid was **sterile** (did not contain any living bacteria), Roux and Yersin injected large amounts of the sterile broth (35 milliliters) into guinea pigs. The guinea pigs died in 5 or 6 days, with many of the same symptoms that would occur if they had been infected with *C. diphtheriae.* Further experiments showed that older cultures (for example, 42 days old) contained even higher levels of toxin. Guinea pigs injected with just 2 milliliters of the broth from the older culture died within 24 hours. Collectively, these experiments showed that the bacteria release a toxin into the culture medium and that this toxin is responsible for most symptoms of the disease. Roux and Yersin further showed that the toxin had attributes of a protein, since boiling the broth destroyed its toxicity. As with much of science, this work led to further questions that would be answered in future investigations.

A TREATMENT FOR DIPHTHERIA

Two of the key questions that would soon be addressed were whether animals could develop immunity to the toxin and whether this knowledge could be used to develop a

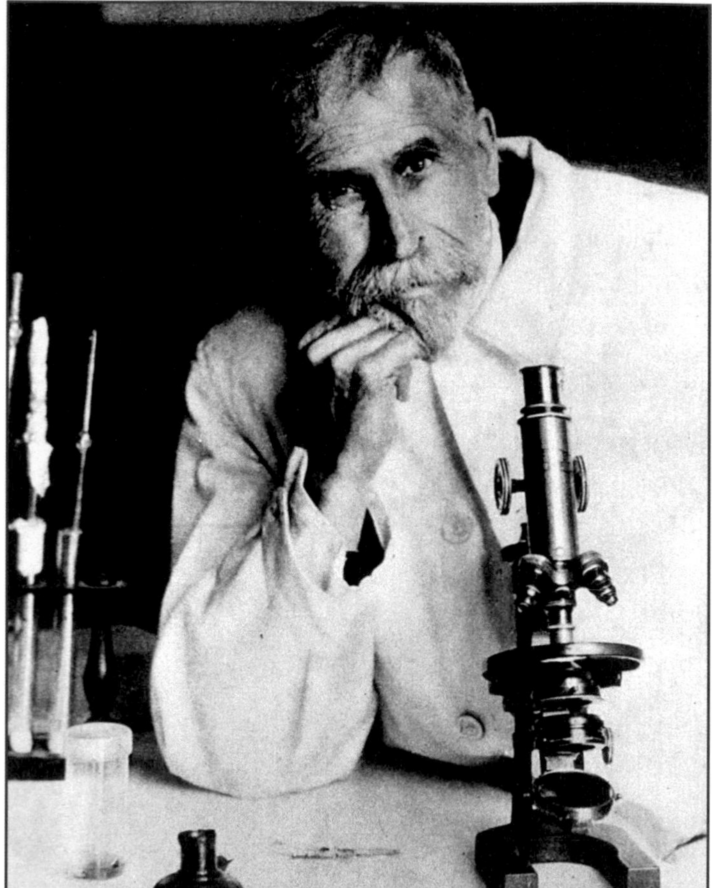

Figure 2.2 Emile Roux, shown here, worked with Alexander Yersin to isolate the toxin produced by *C. diphtheriae*. (National Library of Medicine/U.S. National Institutes of Health)

treatment for diphtheria. In 1890, Emil von Behring, a German scientist at Robert Koch's Institute for Infectious Diseases, reported on work on this topic in a paper entitled "Studies on the Mechanism of Immunity to Diphtheria in Animals." In this paper, Behring reported on experiments in which he immunized animals against diphtheria. He tried several methods. For example, he inoculated guinea pigs with heat-killed *C. diphtheriae* for two weeks, and following those series of inoculations, the guinea pigs were able to resist an otherwise lethal dose of live *C. diphtheriae.* In another set of experiments, he treated cultures of *C. diphtheriae* with iodine for 16 hours to weaken the bacteria. He injected the treated bacteria in guinea pigs; three weeks later, he injected the guinea pigs with bacteria treated with a more dilute solution of iodine. Finally, two weeks later, he injected the guinea pigs with an untreated culture of *C. diphtheriae*, and they survived. In contrast, guinea pigs that were injected with untreated cultures of *C. diphtheriae* and that had not received any injections of the weakened, iodine-treated *C. diphtheriae,* died within a day and a half.[9]

Further experiments by Behring demonstrated that the ability of an animal to resist infection and inactivate the toxin was contained in the blood of the animal. (The active components in the blood are now known to be antibodies.) Additional work in understanding immunity to diphtheria was published by Behring in 1892. He, along with his coauthor Erich Wernicke, described experiments where sheep had been treated so that they became immune to diphtheria. In these experiments, they grew *C. diphtheriae* for four months in laboratory culture, which maximized the amount of toxin produced by these microbes. The culture was then filtered to remove the bacteria and treated with iodine to inactivate the toxin. The treated toxin was injected into sheep, and the blood of these animals was, after a time, found to be capable of inactivating the toxin. The ability of blood from immunized sheep to protect against diphtheria was assayed by testing in guinea pigs. Guinea pigs would be injected with different amounts of sheep serum. The following day, they would be injected with a culture of live diphtheria bacteria. The lower the dose of sheep serum that still protected the guinea pigs against diphtheria, the more potent the sheep serum was. Ultimately, Behring was awarded the Nobel Prize in Medicine in 1901 for his work in developing antitoxin therapy.

This work was further advanced by the German scientist Paul Ehrlich, who developed methods to produce more effective diphtheria antitoxin. He also invented a way of standardizing the potency of the serum in neutralizing diphtheria toxin. In 1894, Ehrlich published his first paper relating to diphtheria, entitled "On the Production and Use of Diphtheria Antiserum." ("Antiserum" and "antitoxin" are synonyms.) Building on the work of Behring, and based on his previous work studying immunity to another toxin, Ehrlich started by injecting goats with dead *C. diphtheriae* and eventually injected the animals with larger and larger doses of live, virulent bacteria.

One of the problems with previous work on testing diphtheria antitoxin was that the assay to determine the potency of the antitoxin was unreliable. The original methods used by Behring relied on injecting the toxin and the antitoxin separately into a guinea pig and determining whether the animal showed any symptoms. However, because individual guinea pigs differed in how quickly they took up the toxin and antitoxin, there was often substantial variation in the outcome from animal to animal, even when the same toxin and antitoxin preparations were used.

Ehrlich's innovation was to mix the toxin and antitoxin prior to injecting them into the guinea pigs. He could then standardize a dose of antitoxin based on its ability to neutralize a standard volume of previously characterized toxin. From this work, he developed the concept of an "immunization unit," the amount of antitoxin that could neutralize the toxin in 1 milliliter of a standard preparation.

Using this information, Ehrlich and his collaborators tested antitoxin preparations on children who had diptheria symptoms in several German hospitals. In all, 220 children were treated with at least 130 units of antitoxin, and 76 percent survived. But more striking was the effect of the timing

Figure 2.3 Paul Ehrlich, shown here, improved upon Emil von Behring's work to develop a more effective diphtheria antitoxin. (National Library of Medicine/U.S. National Institutes of Health)

of the treatments. In cases where the patients had been treated with antitoxin on the first day they developed symptoms, all of them survived, whereas nearly half died if their treatment started five days after their symptoms appeared. It was clear that if antitoxin was going to be used, it would have to be administered early in the course of the disease. In addition, in spite of the progress that had been made in standardizing antitoxin, there was still some variability. For example, Ehrlich determined that preparations of toxin and antitoxin in solution deteriorate over time. Therefore, what was a protective dose of antitoxin initially might no longer be protective some months later.

To further address this issue of standardizing antitoxin, Ehrlich conducted additional experiments, which were published in 1897. In this paper, he determined that a standard preparation, in order to be usable for a long period of time, should be preserved as a powder. When the antitoxin was needed, it could be dissolved in salt water and glycerol, and then injected. When kept as a powder, away from light, heat, and other factors that could cause the antitoxin to deteriorate, it could be preserved for long periods of time. An additional advantage of this method of preserving antitoxin was that samples of the antitoxin, at a standard potency, could be distributed worldwide to ensure that antitoxin preparations everywhere would have the appropriate therapeutic effect.

Erhlich also further developed a method for standardizing an "immunization unit" now defined as the amount of antitoxin needed to neutralize 100 lethal doses of toxin. This could be tested by using toxin standards that contained 100 lethal doses of toxin and determining how much antitoxin solution was required to neutralize the toxin. (Whether a toxin was neutralized was determined by mixing the toxin and antitoxin, and determining whether enough free toxin was still available to kill a 250-gram guinea pig in four to five days.) Although there was still some variability in this test, it provided a consistent enough standard to allow for the development of effective antitoxin therapy around the world.[10] Ehrlich went on to become a corecipient of the Nobel

Prize in Medicine in 1908 for his work related to understanding immunity, which was based, in part, on his experiments involving toxins, including diphtheria toxin.[11]

DIAGNOSTIC TESTS AND DETERMINING THE ROLE OF CARRIERS

Once standardized antitoxin became available as an effective treatment for diphtheria, it became increasingly important to diagnose patients as quickly as possible. This had two benefits: One, rapid treatment with antitoxin was more likely to be curative. Two, rapid detection of individuals with disease would reduce the spread of diphtheria by allowing people who had been in contact with a patient to be observed and rapidly treated if needed.

The diagnostic methods that had been developed in the course of identifying *C. diphtheriae*—namely the injection of bacteria into guinea pigs to look for symptoms—was time consuming and expensive. Therefore, new methods of diagnosis were needed. In New York City, starting in 1892, diphtheria was diagnosed by swabbing the throat of a patient with a suspected case of the disease, growing the bacteria from the swab in culture, and determining if the organisms present looked like *C. diphtheriae* under the microscope. These new methods for culturing bacteria revealed the presence of substantial numbers of people who harbored *C. diphtheriae* without showing symptoms of disease. The existence of so-called "carriers" had already been demonstrated by Loeffler, but the extensive testing in New York City showed how widespread this phenomenon was. These individuals were called carriers, and it was apparent that these carriers could spread diphtheria to others. This clarified how some people who had not been in contact with someone showing symptoms of the disease sometimes developed diphtheria. Apparently, these patients had been in contact with carriers of *C. diphtheriae* and became ill as a result. Consequently, there were attempts to quarantine carriers, but the number of carriers was so high this was not practical. Complete control of diphtheria therefore required improved methods of treatment and, ultimately, methods for prevention.[12]

PREDICTING SUSCEPTIBILITY TO DIPHTHERIA

In 1913, while working in Austria, Bela Schick developed a method to determine if a person has immunity to diphtheria. He injected a small amount of diphtheria toxin (one-fiftieth of a lethal dose for a guinea pig) under the skin of a patient. If a person was immune, no reaction would result. This was called a negative **Schick test.** If the person was susceptible to the toxin, he or she would develop a reddish bump 10 to 20 millimeters in diameter, which would last 7 to 10 days. This would be considered a positive Schick test, and it meant that the person was susceptible to developing diphtheria. This test proved useful to determine susceptibility to diphtheria in different age groups (typically young children were most susceptible). It would also prove valuable, once a diphtheria vaccine was developed, to help determine which individuals could benefit from vaccination.[13]

THE DEVELOPMENT OF AN EFFECTIVE VACCINE

Frequently, vaccines are developed using whole killed pathogens or whole live strains of the pathogens that had been weakened. However, since it was clear that all or nearly all of the symptoms of diphtheria were the result of the toxin produced by *C. diphtheriae*, most of the focus in vaccine development was on using the toxin itself as the sole component of the vaccine. There was initially some work done in animals, testing a vaccination with whole, but dead, *C. diphtheriae* cells. However, the potential for side effects and complications was greater using a whole-cell vaccine, and the use of preparations of toxin alone appeared to induce adequate immunity. Consequently, subsequent vaccination experiments involved the purification of toxin from cultures of *C. diphtheriae*, followed by some type of treatment to inactivate the toxin. One of the early animal experiments (by Behring) used an iodine compound to **attenuate**, or reduce the potency of, the toxin; this attenuated toxin was then tested for its usefulness as a vaccine. Although this strategy showed some promise, it apparently was not as safe or effective as other methods, and consequently it was abandoned.

Another strategy for vaccination was based on the observation that animals could be immunized against diphtheria using a mixture of toxin and antitoxin. This observation came from the work of Paul Ehrlich, who showed that mixing toxin and antitoxin together, and then injecting them into animals, gave a more accurate measure of the potency of the antitoxin, as compared with injecting the two substances separately into the animals. Subsequently, it was demonstrated that these animals had developed some immunity to the toxin, and this led to further work on using this mixture for vaccinating humans.

In fact, the first vaccine for diphtheria used on a large scale in humans consisted of a mixture of diphtheria toxin with diphtheria antitoxin. The idea was that the toxin was present, so people injected with the mixture could develop immunity to the toxin. Yet, since the toxin was bound to antibodies from the antitoxin, the toxin could not enter cells and do damage. A human antitoxin-toxin vaccine was produced by Emil von Behring in 1913 and was tested on a limited group of people. Shortly thereafter, in 1914, William Park, in the Health Department of New York City, tested a group of 700 children at diphtheria hospitals in the city using the Schick test, followed by immunization with antitoxin-toxin mixtures for those who were susceptible. This trial showed that it was possible to produce immunity to diphtheria through vaccination. By 1921, 52,000 children in New York City were tested for immunity using the Schick test, and those found to be susceptible to diphtheria were given vaccinations with toxin-antitoxin mixtures. This vaccine used actual, functional toxin. Consequently, if the antitoxin became inactivated or the amount of antitoxin was not sufficient to bind to all the toxin, there was a danger that the vaccination could, itself, cause symptoms of the disease. In fact, there were occasional reports of illness caused by improperly prepared mixtures of toxin and antitoxin.[14]

THE DEVELOPMENT OF A TOXOID VACCINE

Ultimately, a vaccine that was simpler to prepare, and that did not contain functional toxin, was developed by Gaston Ramon, who did this work at the Pasteur Institute in Paris, France, during the 1920s. This vaccine consisted of the diphtheria **toxoid**, which was diphtheria toxin that had been treated with heat and the chemical formaldehyde so that it was permanently inactivated.

Two major breakthroughs were required for the development of this safe, stable, simple vaccine, and Ramon was responsible for both of them. The first development was an improved assay for the toxin and then the inactivated toxin (the toxoid). Previous assays to test the potency of toxin (or antitoxin) relied on animal tests, with the end point being that the animal either survived or died. However, the result of Ramon's work was ultimately a vaccine containing a permanently inactivated toxin, so the animal tests would not be useful. In the course of testing diphtheria antitoxin for potency, he noticed that mixtures of toxin and antitoxin in a test tube developed flecks that looked liked cotton dust. He called this a flocculation test (*flocon* is "cotton dust" in French). Importantly, he also noticed that these flecks were most pronounced when the proportions of toxin and antitoxin were matched exactly. This gave him a way to measure the amount of toxin and antitoxin precisely without relying on animal tests. This was crucial when he developed the vaccine consisting of the permanently inactivated diphtheria toxin (the toxoid). Since the toxoid was not harmful, he needed a test that was not based on an animal living or dying after exposure to this substance.

The second development necessary to produce a safer, more effective vaccine was a method for uniformly preparing a permanently inactivated, yet immunity-stimulating vaccine. As is frequently the case in science, a combination of a prepared mind and luck was involved. Ramon was initially trying to develop a method for preserving the toxin preparations so they would remain a useful standard to assay his preparations of antitoxin. Frequently, the toxin solutions would become contaminated with bacteria and therefore be unusable. He had previous experience using formaldehyde as a disinfectant, so he initially tried adding formaldehyde at a concentration of 1 part formaldehyde to 2,000 parts toxin to his toxin preparations. The formaldehyde worked well as a preservative in preventing the growth of bacteria. However, he also determined that the formaldehyde had inactivated the toxin. While this result could have been interpreted as a failure, fortunately for humanity, Ramon did not scrap the use of formaldehyde, but instead conducted further tests. Importantly, he found that the formaldehyde-treated toxin (the toxoid) still reacted in the flocculation test, indicating that that toxoid was still capable of being bound by antibodies, and therefore he could determine how much toxoid was present in a solution.

Ramon then conducted a vaccination trial with the toxoid in guinea pigs. He injected guinea pigs with a dose of the toxoid, and then a second dose after one month. When these guinea pigs were subsequently given a dose of diphtheria toxin that would normally be sufficient to kill 1,000 guinea pigs, the animals survived.

Ramon further tested the toxoid by injecting it under his skin, and he noted no serious effects. This encouraged him, in concert with coworkers, to conduct further tests in humans. Children living in an area of France where diphtheria was occurring were given a Schick test. Those who were positive (and therefore susceptible to diphtheria) were given an injection of diphtheria toxoid, followed by a second injection 20 days later (similar to the protocol that he had used with the guinea pigs). None of the 102 children treated developed diphtheria, whereas 48 of 1,400 untreated children in that area did develop diphtheria. These tests, and others, confirmed the safety and the efficacy of the toxoid Ramon had developed.

Ramon had also made a couple of other observations that helped make vaccination simpler and more effective. In the course of vaccinating horses to produce antitoxin, he noticed that the horses occasionally developed infections at the site of the injection. Surprisingly, it seemed that the bacteria causing the infection aided in the immune response because horses that had these infections typically produced more potent

PHARMACEUTICAL COMPANIES AND DRUG REGULATION

With the development of diphtheria antitoxin, it became clear that to develop therapeutics in sufficient quantity to treat many people, large companies would need to be involved and that the potential for financial gain was significant. Paul Ehrlich and Emil von Behring were heavily involved in the basic research that led to the development of effective diphtheria antitoxin. They did not, however, have the financial resources to produce antitoxin on a large scale. Initially, Behring had an agreement with the pharmaceutical company Hoechst to split the profits from the antitoxin. However, they were not able to develop an assay for standardizing the product, so Ehrlich was brought in under an agreement where he would share the profits. Shortly thereafter, Behring met with Ehrlich and told him that he would help Ehrlich get his own state institute for doing research, and since, as a director, he would not be eligible to receive royalties, Ehrlich should sign away his royalty rights. In the end, Behring was not able to start the state institute for Ehrlich

antitoxin. This led Ramon to believe that the addition of a substance (now called an **adjuvant**) might increase the ability of the body to react to the injected toxin. He tried a number of substances and eventually found that sterile tapioca (a starch found in the root of the cassava plant and an ingredient in some types of pudding) was quite effective in enhancing immunity to the diphtheria toxoid. Tapioca is not currently used, but other adjuvants are an important component of modern vaccines.

In the same set of experiments, Ramon also tested a mixture of toxoids for both diphtheria and tetanus as a possible vaccine. He discovered that animals injected with this mixture

even though he had already signed away his royalties from the vaccine, leaving Behring rich (earning close to 2 million German marks between 1884 and 1914, equivalent to about 100 million current U.S. dollars)[15] and leaving Ehrlich very much embittered.

The development of large-scale pharmaceutical products was not without its problems. For example, in the United States in 1901, diphtheria antitoxin was collected from a horse that was unknowingly ill with tetanus. A total of 13 children in St. Louis, Missouri died from tetanus as a consequence of receiving the tainted diphtheria antitoxin. A similar incident occurred in Camden, New Jersey that same year, and these tragedies led to the passing of a bill called the Biologics Control Act in 1902. This law regulated the production of biological substances, like antitoxin, and ultimately led to oversight by the Food and Drug Administration of drug production in the United States.[16]

produced high levels of immunity to both toxins. This led to the development of modern vaccines—such as diphtheria, tetanus, and pertussis (DTaP) vaccine—that simultaneously protect against multiple pathogens.[17]

SUBSEQUENT CHANGES IN THE INCIDENCE OF DIPHTHERIA

In colonial America, diphtheria frequently devastated whole communities. For example, in 1735, in Hampton Falls, New Hampshire, approximately 40 percent of the children under the age of 10 died from diphtheria in that single year. As late as 1892, approximately 1 percent of the articles in the world's medical literature were about diphtheria, indicating the importance of this disease to the medical community. Ninety years later, fewer than 0.01 percent of the articles in the medical literature described diphtheria, an indication of the success of medical treatment in reducing the threat from diphtheria and therefore reducing the need for new reports of the effects of medical intervention.[18]

A further example of the seriousness of diphtheria in the nineteenth century comes from the following description:

> Dr. H.D. Paine, of Albany, NY gives the following account of an epidemic of diphtheria which he witnessed during five months, from September, 1858 to February, 1859: "Some idea of the grave nature of this sickness may be gathered from the fact that, since the breaking out of the disease, few, if any, less than 250 deaths therefrom have occurred in the city (Albany) and its immediate neighborhood. [According to the 1860 census, the population of Albany, NY was 62,367 people.] The victims have been almost exclusively children and young persons. In 15 families, there had been in each two deaths; in four families there were in each three deaths, and 104 children had been swept away by the pestilence."[19]

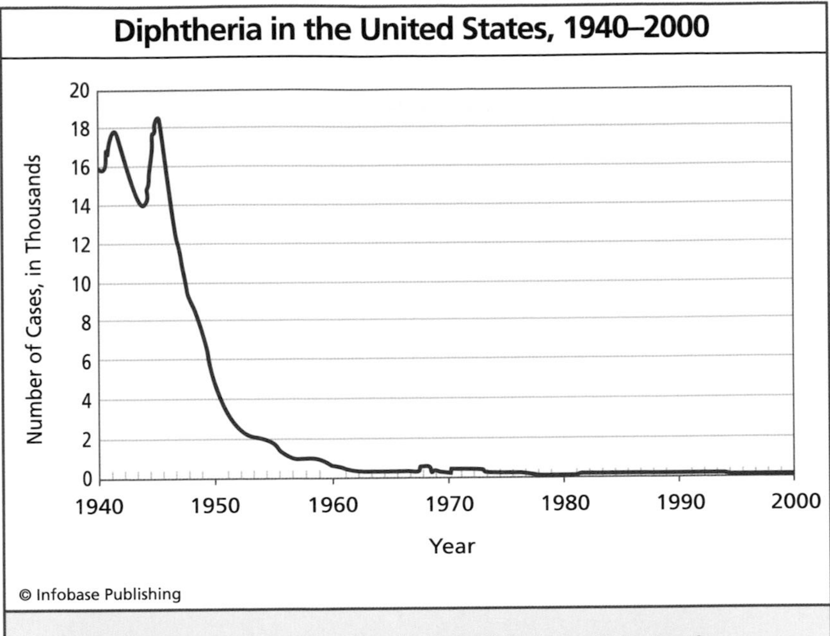

Figure 2.4 Diphtheria cases in United States. Note the dramatic reduction in cases following the approval of the diphtheria vaccine in 1949.

With the development of effective treatments by around 1900, and widespread vaccination by the 1940s, diphtheria became increasingly uncommon in industrialized nations. However, it was estimated that there were still more than 1 million cases of diphtheria and 50,000 to 60,000 deaths per year during the early 1970s. With further efforts to enhance vaccination coverage in less developed countries starting in the 1970s, the number of cases of diphtheria declined to fewer than 100,000 by 1980, and the number of deaths due to diphtheria is now 5,000 or less worldwide in most years.[20,21]

However, during the 1990s, there was a massive outbreak of diphtheria in the countries of the former Soviet Union, with over 150,000 cases and 5,000 deaths during that decade. This

Table 2.1 Chronology of Key Events in the History of Diphtheria

- Seventh century B.C. First possible report of diphtheria by Hippocrates.
- Second century A.D. Likely account of diphtheria by Aretaeus.
- Fifth and sixth centuries A.D. Additional reports of diphtheria.
- 1500s. Reports of diphtheria epidemics in Spain.
- 1500s to 1900s. Repeated outbreaks of diphtheria around the world.
- 1883. Edwin Klebs identifies the diphtheria bacterium.
- 1884. Fredrick Loeffler isolates the diphtheria bacterium.
- 1892. Emil von Behring shows the efficacy of diphtheria antitoxin in treating disease.
- 1897. Paul Ehrlich develops methods for determining the potency of antitoxin.
- 1913. Emil von Behring first tests antitoxin/toxin mixtures for vaccination.
- 1913. Bela Schick develops a test that indicates whether a person is susceptible to diphtheria.
- 1923. Gaston Ramon develops a toxoid vaccine that is the basis for modern diphtheria vaccines.
- 1930s to 1940s. Widespread use of diphtheria vaccine eliminates the disease from most of the world.
- 1990s. Reemergence of diphtheria in the former Soviet Union.
- Twenty-first century. Complete sequence of *C. diphtheriae* determined, new strategies for using diphtheria toxin to treat cancer and other diseases developed. Continued concerns about new diphtheria epidemics as human population grows and wars and other social disruptions limit access to health care.

unfortunate event shows the need for constant vigilance about vaccination and other public health measures, even for diseases that have become relatively uncommon.

3

How Does *Corynebacterium diphtheriae* Cause Disease?

A 70-year-old woman was admitted to a hospital in England. She complained of a sore throat and difficulty swallowing. When she was examined, she had swollen lymph nodes in her neck and was dehydrated. She was given fluids and antibiotics. A few days later, she began to expel liquids through her nose when she attempted to swallow. A throat swab demonstrated C. diphtheriae, *so she was treated with a different antibiotic and her symptoms resolved. About three months later, she reported muscle weakness and a loss of sensation. She was diagnosed with nerve damage caused by diphtheria toxin. With physical therapy, she eventually regained nearly full function.*[1]

Imagine that there is a virus that can infect you and change your personality from a mild-mannered, socially respectable person, to a toxin-spewing monster. While we humans are safe from such a fate, there is a virus (phage B) with these properties that can infect *C. diphtheriae.* In fact, this bacterium can only act as a human pathogen if it, in turn, is parasitized by this bacterial virus. A bacterial virus is known as a **bacteriophage**, and it only infects microbes like *C. diphtheriae.* Typically, a bacterial virus docks on the surface of a bacterial cell and injects its genetic material into the bacterium. At this point, the viral genetic material converts the bacterium into a virus production factory. Alternatively, the virus can insert its genetic material into the DNA of the bacterium and become part of its host. This latter strategy is the one adopted by the virus that infects *C. diphtheriae*. These viruses also have the ability to sense when the cell they are living in comes on hard times. Under those conditions, the virus can extract itself from the genome, break out of the bacterial cell, and go on to infect new cells.

What selective advantage might there be for the virus to carry a toxin-producing gene? Under conditions where people are not vaccinated or do not have access to medical care (the situation until well into the middle of the twentieth century or later in most of the world), *C. diphtheriae* containing the virus probably had a selective advantage. Toxin-producing strains may be capable of growing to a larger population in the body and may be more likely to be effectively transmitted to other people. Since all of the toxin-producing bacteria contain the virus, the virus would be transmitted as well.

Interestingly, with the use of a vaccine that specifically targets the toxin, there is now a selection against *C. diphtheriae* that is infected with the virus. In countries like the United States with widespread vaccination, few strains of virus-infected, toxin-producing *C. diphtheriae* are found in the population. However, it appears that enough toxin-producing strains are present, even in countries with widespread vaccination, that if vaccination levels decline, diphtheria can reemerge as a major problem, as happened in the 1990s in the former Soviet Union.

TOXIN PRODUCTION AND ITS EFFECTS

The study of diphtheria toxin led to the first clear understanding of the molecular details of how a bacterial toxin acts in cells. It was known as early as 1962 that diphtheria toxin interfered with the ability of human cells to make proteins. Since protein

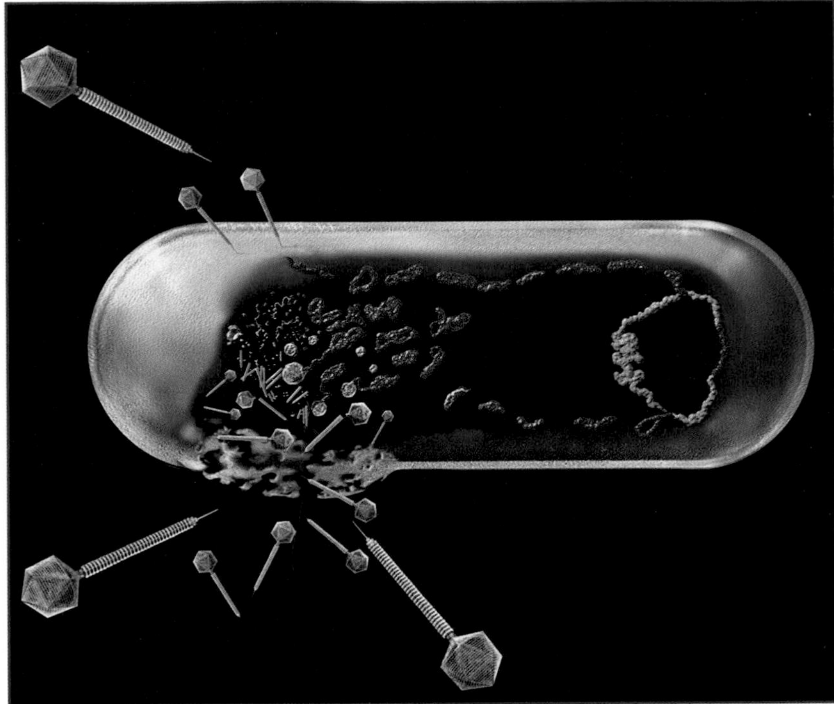

Figure 3.1 Bacteriophages use a bacterium (yellow) to reproduce, using one of two processes. In the lytic process (left), the bacteriophage's DNA quickly produces new bacteriophages that burst forth from the bacterium, killing it in the process (lower left). The lysogenic process (right) is the process used by bacteriophages that infect *C. diphtheriae*. Here, the viral DNA are incorporated into a bacterial DNA loop (green), remaining dormant the bacterium reproduces. This incorporated DNA can later start a lytic cycle. (© Russell Kightley / Photo Researchers, Inc.)

synthesis is an essential function for cells, shutting down this process destroys them. In 1967, a study by a scientist in Switzerland zeroed in on the exact mechanism by which the diphtheria toxin exerts its effects. The researcher used rabbit cells that had been broken open and treated so that the components of the cell essential to making proteins were active. He then added diphtheria toxin to this protein-making system and determined which specific factor was inactivated by the toxin. He determined that it was a cellular protein, called **elongation factor 2** (EF-2), that was inactivated. EF-2 is normally involved in allowing protein chains to grow as they are made in the cell. Interfering with that function prevents protein synthesis and ultimately results in cell death.[2] Further

EVIDENCE THAT A VIRUS CAUSES *C. DIPHTHERIAE* TO GO BAD

Data supporting the strange observation that a viral infection was necessary for *C. diphtheriae* to become a pathogen began accumulating in the 1920s, when it was determined that there were nonpathogenic strains of *C. diphtheriae* that appeared nearly identical to the strains that caused disease. However, these strains did not produce toxin, and therefore, they did not cause diphtheria.

It was also demonstrated during the 1920s that toxin-producing strains could be converted to non-toxin-producing strains, and these strains were permanently rendered avirulent (unable to cause disease). In 1951, a researcher at the University of Washington Medical School in Seattle, Washington, first demonstrated that avirulent strains of *C. diphtheriae* could be converted to pathogenic, toxin-producing strains when these bacteria were incubated with a bacterial virus (called phage B).[3]

Initially, it was not clear what role the bacterial virus played in this conversion; did the virus simply kill bacterial cells that did not produce toxin or did the virus actually carry toxin-producing genes? Further work, starting in 1953, showed that the bacterial virus did not select toxin-producing mutants. Rather, the virus actually contains the toxin gene.[4]

work showed exactly how diphtheria toxin inactivates EF-2. The toxin adds a chemical, called ADP-ribose, to EF-2. The addition of ADP-ribose to EF-2 abolishes the function of EF-2, and, consequently, the ability of the cell to make proteins.

One reason diphtheria toxin is so potent is that it is an **enzyme**, so it can inactivate many molecules of the EF-2 protein. In fact, a single molecule of diphtheria toxin is sufficient to kill a human cell.[5] One of the interesting aspects of the action of diphtheria toxin is that it specifically binds to a modified amino acid in the EF-2 protein called **diphthamide**. This modified amino acid is apparently found only at this one site in this single protein. Bacteria, like *C. diphtheriae*, lack EF-2 (and diphthamide) and consequently, they are not harmed by the toxin they produce. In addition, the toxin is secreted in an inactive form by the bacterial cell, providing further protection from self-intoxication.

Additional research demonstrated that diphtheria toxin must be cut into two pieces to become active. One section (designated "A") is the active portion, which actually does the damage inside the cell. A second section (designated "T") allows the toxin to enter the **cytoplasm**, the cellular material of the cell. The third section (denoted with a "B") is the binding portion, which allows the toxin to latch onto the surface of cells with the appropriate surface molecules. The activity of the two portions of the toxin was determined by using mutant strains of bacteria that produced inactive toxins. One mutant produced a toxin that could not bind to eukaryotic cells. The other mutant produced a toxin that could bind to cells but could not alter EF-2. When the two mutant, inactive toxins were mixed together under conditions where they could be cut into two sections, the cell-binding portion from the one mutant toxin was able to combine with the active region of the other mutant toxin. The result was an active toxin, which demonstrated that the toxin consisted of two pieces, each with a very different function.

HOW DOES THE TOXIN ENTER CELLS?

The previous work made it clear how the toxin damaged cells, but it was not yet clear how the toxin bound to specific cells and how the toxin actually entered the cells. Further experiments showed that two specific proteins on the surface of human cells bound to the "B" portion of the toxin. Binding of the toxin to the receptors induces a normal cellular process called **receptor-mediated endocytosis**. This process results in the toxin being brought into the cell in a small membrane-bound bag called a vesicle. Once inside the cell, the vesicle becomes acidic, and this causes the toxin to change shape. Another section of the toxin, the "T" domain, plays a critical role here. This shape change causes the "T" domain to insert into the vesicle membrane, which, in turn, allows the "A" portion of the toxin to separate from the rest of the toxin and to exit into the cytoplasm, where it can then inactivate EF-2. Once the vesicle enters the cell, there is no way to reverse the damage caused by the toxin. Antibodies cannot touch it, and there are not yet any drugs available that can interfere with the action of the toxin at this point.[6] This is why early treatment of diphtheria is so critical.

Why does the toxin particularly damage cells in the throat, heart, and nervous system? There is not a complete answer yet, but one explanation is that these cell types have more receptors for the toxin, and consequently, they are more likely to bind to the toxin and internalize it.

THE REGULATION OF TOXIN PRODUCTION

Bacteria that produce virulence factors, like toxins, typically produce those factors only when they are in an environment that provides what they require to survive and reproduce. There is logic to this observation, as it takes quite a bit of energy to produce toxin proteins, and, in the case of the diphtheria toxin, up to 5 percent of the protein that *C. diphtheria* produces in the body is the toxin. If the toxin is produced when this microbe is

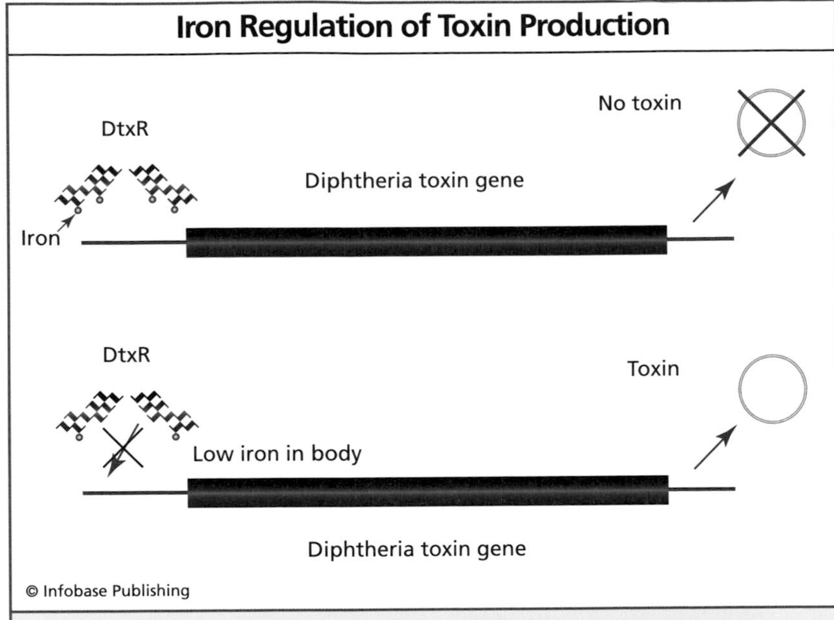

Figure 3.2 The presence of iron regulates toxin production in *C. diphtheriae*. When there is a substantial amount of iron in the environment, the diphtheria toxin repressor (DtxR) protein binds to a region of DNA near the diphtheria toxin gene. This prevents the production of diphtheria toxin. Inside the human body, iron levels are low inside the bacterium; consequently, DtxR cannot bind iron, and it cannot bind to the DNA near the toxin gene. As a result, diphtheria toxin is made.

outside the body, it will waste a tremendous amount of energy, since the toxin probably does not help this organism survive in the environment. Wasting a large amount of energy would make *C. diphtheriae* less likely to survive, so there would be a strong selective pressure to assure that the organism can sense when it is inside the body, and therefore, when it would be appropriate to make the toxin.

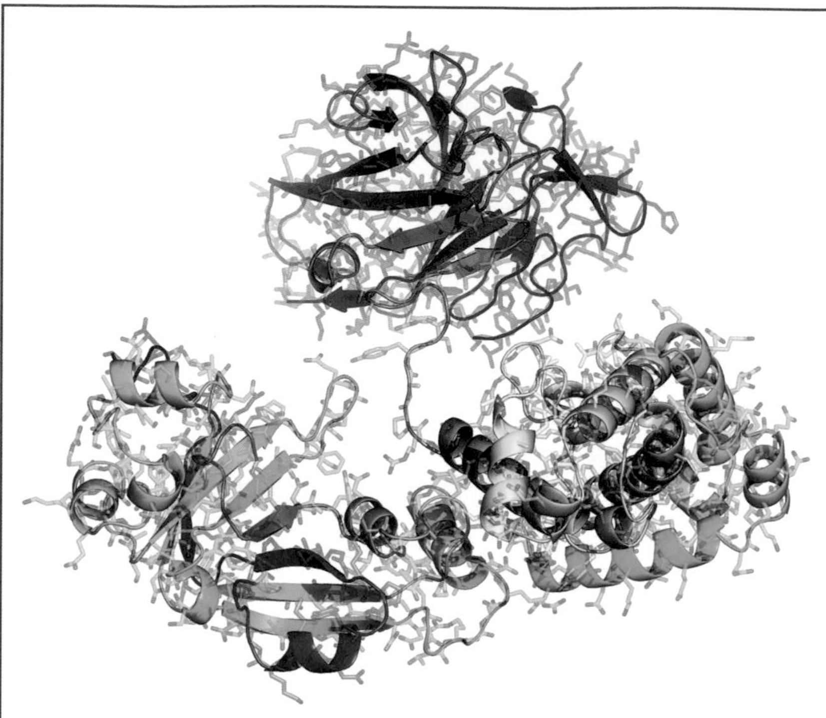

Figure 3.3 This is a molecular model of the diphtheria toxin. The toxin consists of three regions. The "B" region (red) binds to the host cell. The "T" region (green) aids in the movement of the toxin into the host cell's cytoplasm. The "A" region (blue) is the active part of the toxin that interferes with metabolic reactions within the cell, causing diphtheria's signs and symptoms. (© Laguna Design / Photo Researchers, Inc.)

Consequently, the question about regulating toxin production comes down to how *C. diphtheriae* senses that it is in a human body. Different pathogens recognize different cues; some respond to body temperature, some to the availability, or lack thereof, of particular nutrients. The latter situation is the case for *C. diphtheriae*, which recognizes that it is in the body based on a low availability of iron. Although there is a substantial amount of iron inside our bodies, most of it is tightly bound to proteins (like hemoglobin) and is therefore not readily accessible to bacteria.

In the case of *C. diphtheriae*, the production of toxin is regulated by a separate gene called ***dtx*R** (diphtheria toxin repressor). This gene is active in the presence of high iron concentrations; under those conditions, *dtx*R prevents the toxin from being produced. As the iron concentration drops, *dtx*R can no longer stop the toxin protein from being produced. How this toxin regulation occurs is understood in some detail.

The *dtx*R gene produces the DtxR protein. This protein teams up to form a two-part unit. This complex of two DtxR proteins can bind four iron molecules. When bound to iron, the DtxR protein changes shape, and the protein–iron complex binds to DNA near the toxin gene. The bound DtxR protein prevents the toxin gene from functioning, since DtxR binds to a region of DNA that needs to be uncovered in order for the toxin gene to make toxin.

If the concentration of iron drops, the DtxR protein cannot bind iron. Consequently, it cannot bind to DNA and prevent the toxin gene from functioning. As a result, the toxin is produced. Therefore, the DtxR protein is an iron sensor. Low iron correlates with being inside the human body; under those conditions, the DtxR protein is inactive and the toxin gene makes diphtheria toxin.

The DtxR protein itself is apparently produced at relatively similar amounts, regardless of the environmental conditions, so it is always available for regulation.[7] The DtxR protein also regulates a number of other genes that are involved in controlling iron uptake. For example, DtxR regulates the expression of a protein that captures iron from the environment and another protein that strips iron from hemoglobin in red blood cells. As with the toxin, these proteins are only produced when iron levels in the cell are low. This is critical for *C. diphtheriae*, as excess iron can lead to damage from reactive oxygen compounds. Mutation of the *dtx*R gene makes *C. diphtheriae* more susceptible to oxygen damage, consistent with a role for this gene in both toxin regulation and in metering the iron content in the cell.[8] However, these *dtx*R mutants are viable, showing that this gene is not essential for survival of the microbe. These mutants also produce toxin whether or not iron is present in the medium, further confirming the role of DtxR as a protein controlled by the level of iron in the environment.[9]

Considering the role of iron in inducing toxin production in the body, it is interesting to note that one common treatment for the disease in the nineteenth century was the application of iron compounds to the throat. This was claimed to reduce swelling. Although most treatments of the time were of dubious value, one wonders if these applications of iron might have increased the iron concentration surrounding the bacteria to the extent that, at least temporarily, toxin production was reduced.

SITES WHERE *C. DIPHTHERIAE* GROWS IN THE BODY

In developed countries, *C. diphtheriae* is almost exclusively a respiratory pathogen. The organism can colonize a variety of sites in the respiratory tract, including the nose, the throat, and the bronchial passages further down in the lungs. It is not yet clear exactly how *C. diphtheriae* binds to the cells in the respiratory tract, but several surface proteins on the bacteria have been identified as possible **adhesins** (surface proteins that allow binding to other cells). It is also not clear exactly what molecules on the surface of the human cells are binding sites for the bacteria.

In tropical countries, and occasionally in temperate regions, *C. diphtheriae* can also cause skin infections. These skin infections typically occur as non-healing ulcers. The toxin produced by organisms in the skin is apparently not readily absorbed into the body, so there are rarely systemic signs of disease. The prolonged exposure to low levels of toxin from a skin lesion can induce high levels of immunity, and this might explain why respiratory diphtheria is less common in the tropics. It is not clear why cutaneous diphtheria is more common in the tropics, but one possibility might be the more frequent presence of wounds or sores in the skin of people living in the tropics. *C. diphtheriae* normally can establish a skin infection only at the site of a preexisting wound. Some other locations in the body have also been reported as sites of *C. diphtheriae* infection, including the ear canal, the surface of the eye, and the vagina.

C. DIPHTHERIAE VIRULENCE FACTORS

Aside from diphtheria toxin, relatively little has been learned about the other virulence factors of this organism. Recent developments have started to shed some light on these virulence factors, however. In particular, the sequence of the complete genome of *C. diphtheriae* has revealed a number of possible genes that may aid this microbe in making a living inside the human body.[10] Further study into the function of these genes, and their role in the disease process, may allow for the development of novel treatments and new strategies for preventing diphtheria.

4

How Is Diphtheria Treated?

A young toddler, 1½ years old, went to the hospital with a swollen neck and repeated seizures. He was diagnosed with diphtheria and treated with diphtheria antitoxin and antibiotics. His condition improved, and he went home. Nine days later, he developed swelling over his entire body. Further examination determined that he had an inflammation of his kidneys and heart, probably as a result of his diphtheria infection. He was treated with a drug designed to remove excess water from his body and another drug intended to reduce the protein content of his urine. After more than a week in the hospital, his condition improved and he was released.

About a week later, the child developed muscle weakness in his arms and legs. Further examination showed that his nerves had been damaged, and he required the use of a ventilator to assist his breathing for more than two weeks. A week after the onset of the muscle weakness, he showed signs of liver damage. Ultimately, he recovered completely, but only after a great deal of pain and suffering and substantial expense for his medical care. He had never been vaccinated against diphtheria.[1]

The first step in treatment of diphtheria is appropriate diagnosis. As with many areas of medical science, diagnosis has improved substantially in recent years. Once a diagnosis of diphtheria has been made, quick treatment is required. Treatment consists of several steps: airway support, antibiotics to eliminate the bacteria, and antitoxin to bind any free toxin. In rare cases, such as the case study above, the toxin can cause widespread damage to the tissues and organs that results in the need for extensive medical care.

DIAGNOSIS OF DIPHTHERIA

An initial diagnosis is normally made based on clinical signs of diphtheria. Because diphtheria is so rare in developed countries, most physicians there are not accustomed to seeing cases, and this may sometimes delay a diagnosis. The clinical signs of diphtheria include sore throat with the presence of a membrane in the throat, fever, swelling of the neck, and paralysis of the soft

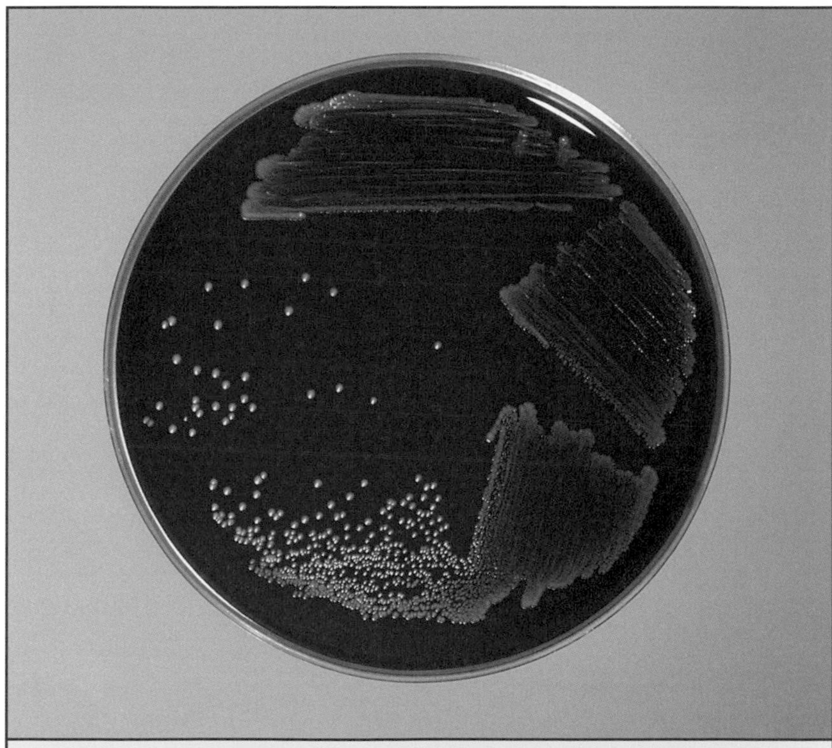

Figure 4.1 Diphtheria cultures are grown on sheep blood agar plates. Colonies of *C. diptheriae*, such as the ones shown here, will appear on this medium within 24 hours. (CDC/Dr. W.A. Clark)

Figure 4.2 In addition to diagnosing diphtheria through cultures, today's lab technicians can use the enzyme-linked immunosorbent assay (ELISA, or enzyme immunoassay) to test for the presence of the diphtheria toxin. Results from an enzyme immunoassay can be obtained in a few hours' time. (Bill Branson/ National Cancer Institute/U.S. National Institutes of Health)

palate. Based on these symptoms, particularly the presence of a sore throat accompanied by the presence of a membrane, a physician would normally begin treatment for diphtheria while waiting for confirmation from the microbiology laboratory. This is critical because early treatment can help avoid complications resulting from the diphtheria toxin damaging the heart and other organs.

In some ways, the standard methods used to identify *C. diphtheriae* in the laboratory have not changed much since the late 1800s, when bacteria from the throats of diphtheria patients were placed on clots of sheep blood. As was the case back then, current methods for identifying a patient with diphtheria start with swabbing the throat of a patient with a suspected case. The swabs are streaked on sheep blood agar plates and another type of medium selective for *C. diphtheriae*, like Tinsdale medium. Once colonies appear (usually within 24 hours), the bacteria are taken from the plate and are stained to determine if the typical microscopic appearance of *C. diphtheriae* is present. A number of staining and biochemical tests are used for definitive identification.[2] There are also commercial kits, such as the API (RAPID) Coryne™ system, which can be used to verify the identity of bacteria thought to be *C. diphtheriae*. Typically these tests require an additional 24 hours after the bacteria have grown on an agar plate.

Other methods are being developed and tested to determine if they can more rapidly and accurately diagnose infections with *C. diphtheriae*. One method that has been tested is an **enzyme immunoassay**. In this technique, an antibody for the diphtheria toxin is bound to the bottom of a plate containing small plastic wells. Broth from a culture of potential *C. diphtheriae* bacteria is added to the well, along with a second antibody that contains a "reporter" molecule. If diphtheria toxin is present, the reporter molecule will give off a signal that can be readily detected. One version of this assay can be completed within three hours after colonies have grown on a plate, allowing for rapid identification of this microbe.[3]

Another important technique that is being used for identification of *C. diphtheriae* is the **polymerase chain reaction** (PCR). This molecular test relies on the unique DNA sequences of *C. diphtheriae*. PCR makes many copies of those unique sequences to the point when they can be readily visualized. PCR requires breaking open the bacterial cells to release their DNA, followed by a set of repeating cycles to make millions of identical units of a particular section of DNA. In the case of *C. diphtheriae*, the toxin gene is frequently the DNA that is amplified, since that gene is unique to this microbe, and the toxin itself is the primary cause of disease.

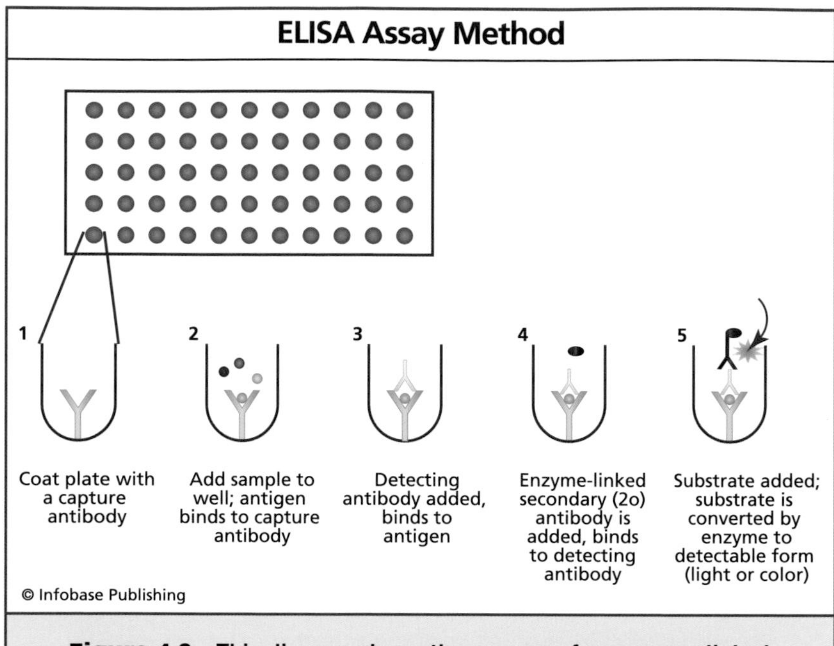

Figure 4.3 This diagram shows the process of an enzyme-linked immunosorbent assay for detecting diphtheria toxin.

The resulting DNA is then visualized either by running it in a gel or determining the production of DNA in a closed tube by measuring its fluorescence.[4]

One example of the utility of PCR for diagnosis comes from researchers at the National Institute of Infectious Diseases in Japan. They studied diagnostic material from a patient who died from suffocation as a consequence of what was initially thought to be a tumor in his throat. Following his death, a throat swab was taken for later analysis and stored in formaldehyde for 53 days. When it was eventually suspected that he may have actually died of diphtheria, PCR was used to amplify DNA from the throat swab. The diphtheria toxin gene was amplified, confirming that the patient actually died of diphtheria. A molecular method like PCR was the only technique that could possibly have allowed that retrospective diagnosis, since the other methods of bacterial identification rely on the growth of bacteria. In this case, the bacteria had been killed by the formaldehyde, so a diagnostic test relying on bacterial growth would not have been successful.[5]

Some of the early symptoms of diphtheria, like sore throat, are associated with many illnesses, meaning that diagnosis of the disease can sometimes be delayed. Yet rapid diagnosis is critical for effective treatment since, once the toxin has entered cells in the body, the damage the toxin causes cannot be undone. Therefore, work will likely continue on developing faster and more effective methods for identifying *C. diphtheriae.*

ILLNESSES AND CONDITIONS THAT CAN BE CONFUSED WITH DIPHTHERIA

Many of diphtheria's symptoms are similar to those of other illnesses, and these illnesses need to be ruled out to aid in the initial diagnosis of the disease. In particular, early in the course of diphtheria, a sore throat may be among the only symptoms, and that is a symptom associated with a variety of other ailments.

For example, mononucleosis often causes a sore throat and may produce a membrane in the throat. However, the membrane in mononucleosis is normally white and does not bleed when it is removed, in contrast with diphtheria, where the membrane typically bleeds when it is scraped and is commonly a gray color.

Streptococcal sore throat, compared with diphtheria, causes a higher fever, a more inflamed throat, and more discomfort when swallowing or eating. Other bacterial infections of the throat typically develop more suddenly; cause a more reddened, inflamed throat; and typically do not produce a membrane. In contrast, diphtheria often develops more slowly, results in a sore throat that is less painful, and leads to the production of a pseudomembrane.

STOPPING THE DIPHTHERIA TOXIN

Once *C. diphtheriae* starts growing in the body, it quickly releases a toxin that will damage tissues, particularly the throat, the heart, and the nerve tissues. As noted above, there is a short window of time between the release of toxin by the bacteria and the toxin being hidden inside cells in the body. Therefore, treatment to bind the toxin before it can cause damage needs to start quickly. The primary method for preventing toxin damage is through the use of diphtheria antitoxin.

Diphtheria antitoxin consists of **blood serum** (the liquid portion of the blood with the cells removed) isolated from a horse. To produce antitoxin, the horse is injected repeatedly with increasing doses of a diphtheria vaccine, and consequently the horse produces high levels of antibody to the diphtheria toxin. These antibodies are present in the horse's blood serum. When this serum is injected into patients with diphtheria, these antibodies bind to the toxin and prevent it from entering cells.

Since antitoxin is produced in horses, and since about 10 percent of patients have an allergic reaction to horse serum, the patients need to be tested to verify they are not allergic before a full dose of antitoxin is used. This is done by injecting a small amount of horse serum under the skin or dropping it on the surface of the eye. If a reaction occurs (redness in the eye or a welt under the skin) then the person must be desensitized by being given a series of increasingly larger doses of the antitoxin prior to being given a full dose. In the United States, because diphtheria is so rare, the antitoxin is currently available only from the Centers for Disease Control and Prevention (CDC) in Atlanta, Georgia.

Based on experiments in animals, it takes about 10 hours from the time diphtheria toxin enters the body, until it does irreversible damage to the organs and tissues. This is the reason that a rapid diagnosis and quick administration of the antitoxin is critical in treating patients.[6]

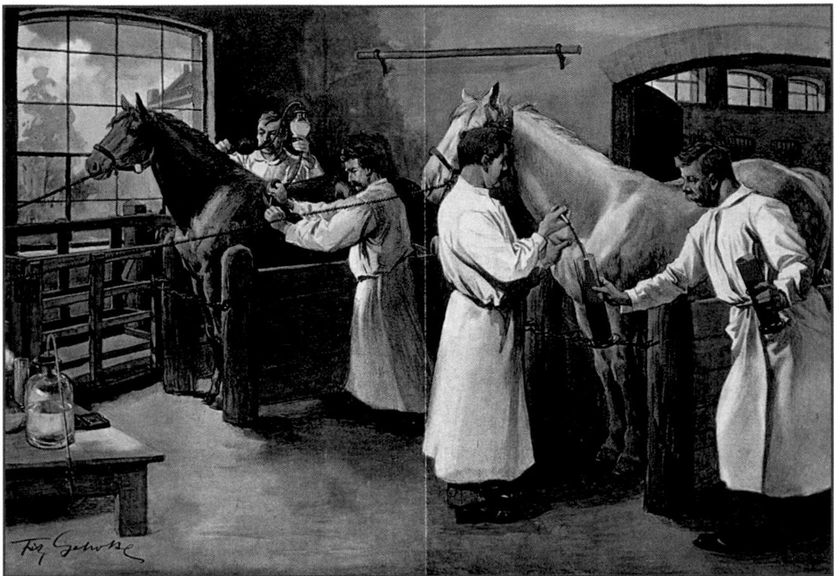

Figure 4.4 This painting from around 1900 shows serum being drawn from inoculated horses, which will be used to make diphtheria antitoxin. Diphtheria antitoxin is still made in this manner, although the development and administration of diphtheria vaccines has reduced the need for antitoxin. (© Jean-Loup Charmet/ Photo Researchers, Inc.)

ELIMINATING TOXIN-PRODUCING BACTERIA

C. diphtheriae is normally susceptible to a number of antibiotics, although there have been some reports of **antibiotic resistance**. Bacteria that are antibiotic resistant are no longer killed or inhibited by commonly used antibiotic medications. Usually, the antibiotics penicillin or erythromycin are used to treat diphtheria. The antibiotic treatment often extends for two weeks to ensure the bacteria are eradicated. Even though a patient under antibiotic treatment may quickly feel better, testing has shown that the bacteria may often be present in

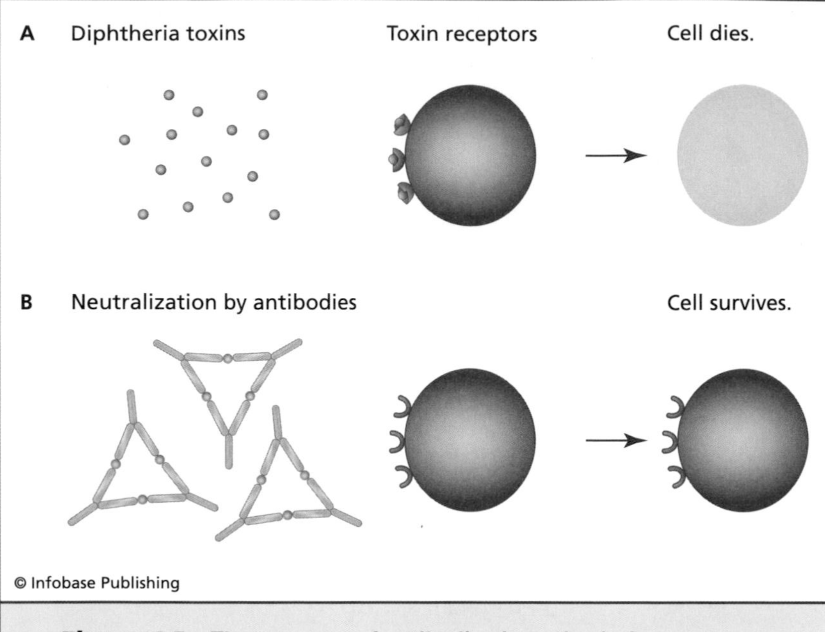

Figure 4.5 The presence of antibodies in antitoxin is a matter of life or death at the cellular level. In panel A, antitoxin is absent, which allows the toxin to bind to the receptors. The toxin is brought into the cell, which causes the cell to die. In panel B, the antibodies present in the antitoxin prevent the toxin from binding to and entering cells. Consequently, the cell survives.

the throat a week or more following treatment. The prolonged treatment with an antibiotic increases the likelihood the bacteria are eradicated and consequently reduces the risk of the transmission of diphtheria to others. Typically, a patient is kept away from other people until two successive throat swabs, taken 24 hours apart, do not show the presence of any *C. diphtheriae.*

TREATING THE SYMPTOMS OF THE DISEASE

The main complications of diphtheria are suffocation, organ damage from the toxin, and partial paralysis. The danger of suffocation is treated through intubation or tracheotomy. **Intubation** involves inserting a plastic tube down the throat into the trachea of the patient to prevent the respiratory tract from being blocked with the pseudomembrane. Tracheotomy is a surgical technique in which a cut is made in the front of the neck and a tube is inserted through the skin into the trachea. Like intubation, this procedure is designed to prevent the respiratory tract from being obstructed. Pierre Bretonneau, who coined the term *diphtheria,* developed tracheotomy as a treatment for this disease.[7]

Organ damage, particularly damage to the heart, is managed by monitoring the patient's heart using an electrocardiogram. If the heart starts beating erratically, drug treatments can be used or a pacemaker can be temporarily implanted. If the heart muscle becomes weak, the drug digitalis can be administered. However, even with heroic treatment, some patients with very serious heart disturbances still die.

For patients with muscle paralysis, physical therapy is used to ensure that muscle function is maintained as the nerves slowly regain function. Generally, full or nearly full function is restored after a period of rehabilitation that may take weeks to months.[8]

Unlike many diseases, a diphtheria infection does not necessarily lead to protective immunity against subsequent infection. Therefore, a critical part of the treatment for a person who has recovered from diphtheria is to ensure that he or she is appropriately vaccinated. The vaccine and vaccine schedules are described in the next chapter.

PREVENTING TRANSMISSION OF DIPHTHERIA FROM A PATIENT

By the late 1890s, it was clear that diphtheria could be contracted from direct contact with bacterial-laden secretions from a patient, or indirectly from *C. diphtheriae* dispersed in the environment when a patient coughed or sneezed. For

(continues on page 70)

A FAMOUS GOYA PAINTING AND DIPHTHERIA

A famous 1812 painting by the Spanish painter Francisco José de Goya shows a man grabbing a young boy around the neck and placing his fingers in the boy's mouth. This painting has sometimes been titled *Curación del Garrotillo* (Treatment of Diphtheria) although that name did not come from Goya himself. The implication was that the man was attempting to treat the young boy's diphtheria by removing the membrane in his throat, perhaps using a utensil that had been heated in the fire in the background of the painting. During Goya's lifetime, there was little available in terms of specific treatments for the disease, aside from the ineffective practice of physical removal of a membrane that was obstructing breathing.

However, a number of features of the painting do not fit that traditional interpretation. For example, there are no obvious tools in the man's hand that might have been used to effect the treatment. In addition, the angle of the child's neck is not appropriate for reaching a membrane in the back of the child's throat. An alternate interpretation of the painting it that it represents a young boy who took a sausage from a blind man, and the man thrust his fingers down the boy's throat to see if he could detect the smell of sausage. This interpretation is based on the discovery of an alternative title for the painting, *El Lazarillo de Tormes*. This title refers to a book from the 1500s that contains the scene shown in the painting. In the book, a blind man has a young helper. At one point, the man asks his assistant to cook a sausage for him on the fire. In the story, the boy steals the sausage, whereupon the blind man puts his fingers in the boy's throat to see if he had eaten the sausage. This is likely the scene

Figure 4.6 Goya's *El Lazarillo de Tormes*, sometimes known as *Curación del Garrotillo* (Treatment of Diphtheria), 1808–1810 (© Erich Lessing/Art Resource, NY)

captured in the painting. However, because diphtheria was so prevalent during the 1800s, it is easy to see why an alternative explanation about the painting, involving this disease, may have come about.

(continued from page 67)

example, diphtheria bacteria could be isolated from pillows and bedding, from a broom used to sweep the floor in rooms used by diphtheria patients, even from the hair of a nurse who attended diphtheria patients. Several experiments demonstrated that the bacteria could survive for days or weeks on environmental surfaces.[9]

Therefore, another important element of diphtheria treatment is to prevent the spread of the disease to people who had contact with a patient. In the United States, the CDC recommends that close contacts of a patient be informed of their exposure to diphtheria and that their nasal passages and throats be swabbed and cultured to see if they have been infected with *C. diphtheriae.* As a precaution, it is also recommended that these individuals be given antibiotics. People with close contact to a patient should be revaccinated if their previous vaccine was more than five years prior to the time they were exposed to the disease. If contacts show any symptoms of diphtheria, antitoxin should be administered promptly and the other methods for treating diphtheria described above should be implemented as well.

HISTORICAL BACKGROUND ON DIPHTHERIA TREATMENT

Prior to the development of antitoxin, which was the first effective treatment for diphtheria, a variety of remedies and techniques were used to treat the disease, and none of them apparently reduced mortality. In fact, a surprisingly honest assessment of medical treatments available in the 1860s stated, "We have no specific remedy for diphtheria . . . The specific disease is not cut short—it is not cured by our remedies; it runs its course, do what we may to prevent it."[10] Examples of common treatments included "two ounces of brandy or four ounces of wine per 24 hours . . . and as much as 20 ounces of brandy . . . within 24 hours." The traditional practice of bloodletting with a scalpel or leeches was used as well. Calomel or other compounds were used to induce diarrhea, with the idea that this treatment would remove poisons from the body. Iron compounds were often applied to the throat of patients, and these treatments were claimed to reduce swelling. *C. diphtheriae* produces toxin only when it detects little iron in the environment, so it is possible that this treatment might have actually had some effect.) Other treatments included the application of a variety of toxic or caustic substances to the throat, including mercury compounds, phenol (carbolic acid), an aspirin-like compound (salicylic acid), a mixture of hydrochloric acid and honey, silver nitrate, copper sulfate, tannic acid, and sulfur. Other therapies included gargling with lead compounds, along with a variety of other potions and remedies. A nourishing diet of "beef-tea and eggs" was also recommended, although one could imagine that, if it was not difficult enough already to swallow as a consequence of diphtheria, the damage to the delicate tissues of the throat by treatment with those compounds might make even the thought of swallowing anything almost unbearable. In addition, with the possible exception of iron compounds, none of these treatments were effective, but it was likely that physicians and their patients were willing to try almost anything to reduce the high death rate from this illness.[11]

5

How Is Diphtheria Prevented?

In 1961, I tended my young cousin while her mother went to work. She was ill with a fever and complained of a sore throat. The next morning she was unable to breathe and began turning blue. An ambulance was called and she was transported to St. Mark's Hospital in North Salt Lake. The doctors there performed a tracheotomy and did everything they could for her, but she passed away that afternoon from diphtheria. Later that week I also became very ill, as did my aunt and another cousin. Although I never became ill enough to be hospitalized, my aunt and cousin were in the hospital by the end of the week. I had been immunized against diphtheria as an infant, but had never had a booster. My case at age 15 was considered mild, but I thought it was awful. Like my young cousin, I suffered from a high fever and experienced difficulty breathing. I survived and have never missed a booster immunization. All of my children and grandchildren also have been fully immunized. My young cousin who passed away at the age of two was not so fortunate. Her mother had never gotten around to getting her vaccinated. My cousin would have survived the attack of diphtheria if she had only been immunized. Her mother and brother both survived and have since become great supporters of immunization. But nothing can bring back little Lois, no matter how much we all wish things had been different.[1]

THE IMPORTANCE OF VACCINATION

Carolyn Hardman's story, above, of her young cousin's death from diphtheria highlights the importance of receiving a vaccination for the disease. The primary method of preventing diphtheria is vaccination of all or nearly all of the population. By the late 1920s, a safe and effective vaccine had been developed. Vaccination against diphtheria eventually became widespread, starting in the 1930s in Canada and in the 1940s in the United States and Europe, and has largely been responsible for the almost complete disappearance of diphtheria in the developed countries of the world.

Currently, most of the vaccines for diphtheria simultaneously protect against diphtheria, tetanus, and pertussis (DTaP vaccine). (Tetanus is caused by the bacterium *Clostridium tetani*; pertussis or whooping cough is caused by the bacterium *Bordetella pertussis.*) Vaccination for diphtheria in the United States currently involves a set of six injections prior to the age of 12. A single booster dose with tetanus, diphtheria, and pertussis (Tdap) is now recommended in adolescents and for adults who did not receive the adolescent booster. This vaccine consists of the diphtheria toxin, which has been attenuated by treatment with heat and formaldehyde. The vaccine also contains tetanus toxin, which has been rendered harmless by a similar treatment process. The vaccine additionally contains inactivated pertussis toxin and, in some cases, other protein components of the bacterium *B. pertussis.* For adults who have had their initial course of shots, a booster is given every ten years with only tetanus toxoid and a lower dose of diphtheria toxoid (Td).[2]

VACCINE SIDE EFFECTS

All medical treatments have some risk associated with them. Although vaccines are generally considered to be very safe, side effects do sometimes occur.[3] For example, with the DTaP vaccine, mild side effects occur in up to one-third of children within a few days of receiving the shot. These side effects include the following:

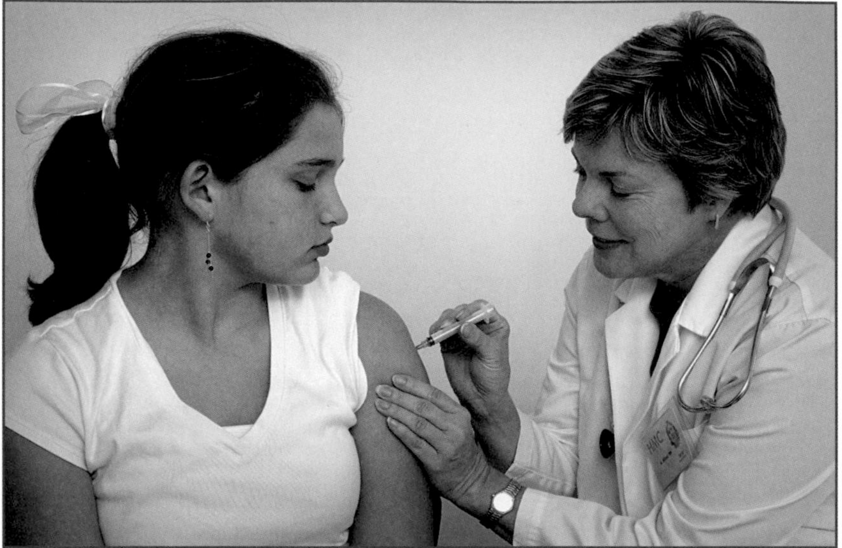

Figure 5.1 The nurse shown here is administering an intramuscular vaccination. Diphtheria vaccinations are given at several points in childhood and periodic boosters are recommended for adults. (CDC/Judy Schmidt)

- fever, along with pain, swelling, and/or redness at the site of injection
- tiredness and fussiness
- swelling of the entire arm (in about 1 child in 30; more often after the fourth or fifth dose of vaccine)
- vomiting (in about 1 child in 50)

Generally these symptoms pass without any treatment or further complications. In some ways they are actually a positive sign, in that they suggest that the immune system is reacting to the vaccine in a way that will engender defense against these diseases.

Moderate side effects are rarer and include the following:

- nonstop crying for three hours or more (1 child in 1,000)

- seizures, jerking, or staring (1 child in 14,000)
- fever above 105°F (1 child in 16,000)

Although serious and of great concern to caregivers, these symptoms normally pass without the need for treatment (beyond the use of a non-aspirin pain reliever to treat fever). Severe reactions to the vaccine are very rare. Severe effects that have been linked to the vaccine include serious allergic reactions, which are reported in less than one case in a million. Other severe ailments that have occurred after vaccination include permanent brain damage and long-term seizures. However, no clear link has been made between the vaccine and these conditions.

Another vaccine (DTwP), which consisted of whole *B. pertussis* cells along with diphtheria and tetanus toxoids, had a higher rate of vaccine side effects (about 26 reports per 100,000 vaccinations versus about 12 per 100,000 with DTaP). Following studies that showed the DTaP vaccine (with acellular pertussis antigens) was effective at preventing these three diseases, DTaP has been recommended for childhood immunization in the United States from the year 2000 onward.[4]

Table 5.1 Recommended DTaP Vaccine Schedule in the United States, 2008[5]

2 months	4 months	6 months	15–18 months	4–6 years	11–12 years	13–18 years	every 10 years
DTaP	DTaP	DTaP	DTaP	DTaP	Tdap	Tdap*	Td**

* 18-year-olds who did not receive the Tdap booster in adolescence, replace one Td with Tdap.

**Adolescents who did not receive booster at 11–12 years or who received Td only should receive Tdap between 13 and 18 years of age, or 5 years after last Td; for adults who did not receive the Tdap booster in adolescence, replace one Td with Tdap.

Source: CDC

VACCINE CONTRAINDICATIONS

Based on an analysis of vaccine side effects, it is recommended that the vaccine *not* be administered in the following cases:

- a child with a moderate or severe illness (the vaccination should wait until he or she recovers)
- a child with a severe allergic reaction to a previous dose of the vaccine
- a child who developed disease of the central nervous system within a week after a previous DTaP vaccination.

Parents should consult with their physician about the advisability of vaccination in the following situations:

- a child who cried for three hours or more following vaccination
- a child who developed a fever of 105°F following vaccination
- a child who had seizures following vaccination[6]

VACCINE SAFETY

While no medical intervention is without some risks, perhaps the best way of evaluating the risk from a diphtheria vaccine is to compare the likelihood of serious harm from taking the vaccine to the likelihood of such harm from not taking the vaccine. Experts infer that without vaccination the United States would annually have approximately 450,000 diphtheria cases and 22,500 deaths (based on approximately 150 cases per 100,000 people prior to the availability of vaccination and a 5 percent mortality rate).

Researchers analyzed side effects linked to the Td vaccine in the United States that were reported to the Vaccine Adverse Event Reporting System (VAERS) between 1991 and 1997.[7] In their analysis, researchers from the Utah Department of

Health, the CDC, and the Food and Drug Administration determined that one death occurred that *may* have been linked to the approximately 73 million doses of vaccine containing diphtheria toxoid that were used during this period. But what would have happened had those doses not been dispensed? Based on an expectation of 150 cases and 7.5 deaths from diphtheria per 100,000 people, one would have expected 5,423 deaths among the 73 million people who had been vaccinated against diphtheria. In addition, a total of 22,500 deaths from diphtheria would have been expected in the 300 million or so residents of the United States per year, since childhood vaccination protects others in the population from diphtheria. Considering that the one death was not definitely caused by the diphtheria vaccination, the relative risk of death without the vaccine may well be greater than 22,500 to 1. The VAERS system collects voluntary reports of vaccine side effects from health care providers, patients, and others. Because the reports are not required, there is the possibility that complications of vaccination may be underreported. However, another study indicated that very serious reactions, such as seizures, were very likely to be entered into the VAERS, suggesting that most of the vaccine-associated deaths would have been reported.[8]

To provide a mechanism for compensating patients who have a serious adverse reaction to vaccination, the United States has established a National Vaccine Injury Compensation Program.[9] Currently, for the DTaP vaccine, the serious complications for which compensation is available include:

- Anaphylaxis or anaphylactic shock within four hours of receiving the shot. This is a severe allergic reaction to the vaccine that can cause death as a result of airway blockage. Based on a study by scientists at research institutions and hospitals on the West Coast of the United States,[10] the risk of anaphylaxis for vaccines containing the diphtheria toxoid is approximately two per one million doses of vaccine. Although serious, if recognized quickly, this reaction can easily be treated in most medical settings.

- Brachial neuritis, a nervous system disorder that normally starts with a deep, severe pain in the arm and shoulder and eventually leads to muscle weakness in the upper body. Based on a study of side effects in infants, it appears that brachial neuritis occurs, in this age group at least, at a rate well below one case per 15 million doses.[11] In most patients, recovery from brachial neuritis begins within a month after symptoms appear, and 90 percent of patients had completely recovered after three years.[12]

As the number of serious vaccine-preventable diseases has declined in developed countries, a perception has arisen among some individuals that vaccines are more dangerous than the diseases they are intended to prevent. There have been claims that certain diseases are associated with specific vaccines. In many cases, these claims have not held up to scrutiny. For example, there have been some concerns about a possible link between vaccines and autism and a particular concern based on the use of a mercury-based preservative, thimerosal, in vaccines. Although current medical and scientific evidence does not support a link between the use of this preservative and autism or other illness, to allay these fears, thimerosal was removed from childhood vaccines in the United States as of 2001.[13] In very rare cases, serious illness can follow vaccination. This indicates that there may be a small number of individuals who are genetically predisposed to react to a component of a vaccine However, public health authorities emphasize that the benefits of vaccination greatly outweigh the risks.[14]

In particular, the DTaP vaccine for children and the Td vaccine for adults are considered by public health experts to be among the safest vaccines, since the vaccines consist of only specific proteins that are involved in causing disease in humans, and not whole microbes. As a result, there are fewer components in the vaccine, thus reducing the risk of side effects.

There is both an element of personal benefit and social good involved in receiving vaccinations for communicable diseases. By having a large proportion of the population vaccinated, an epidemic would be less likely to spread, thereby offering additional protection both to those who are and those who cannot be vaccinated.

VACCINE EFFECTIVENESS

The proportion of people who are protected from diphtheria varies with the number of vaccinations received and the time since the last vaccination. Two methods have been used to measure vaccine effectiveness. In one group of studies, the amount of anti-diphtheria antibody present in the blood is measured and is used as an indication of whether or not an individual would be protected against disease. As one example of this type of study, researchers from several universities in Portugal studied the effect of vaccination on a group of women who were over 30. They found that in the 85 women tested who had at least two previous vaccinations, an additional vaccination produced antibody levels that were protective in all the women.[15]

An example of the second type of study, called a case-control study, included people who developed diphtheria and compared them with a group of matched individuals from the same area who did not develop diphtheria. An example of this type of study was reported by researchers from the Ukraine and the United States during a diphtheria outbreak in the Ukraine in the 1990s. They studied 262 individuals who had developed diphtheria and compared them with 524 control individuals who were the same age and used the same clinic for their medical care. Based on their analysis, they concluded that three vaccinations against diphtheria were protective 98.2 percent of the time; five doses resulted in protection in 99.9 percent of individuals.[16] Summarizing several of these types of studies, the Centers for Disease Control and Prevention reported that three doses of diphtheria toxoid vaccine are 73 to 98 percent effective in preventing diphtheria.[17] In addition, individuals who are vaccinated but still develop disease tend to have milder cases of diphtheria.

EVOLUTION, NATURAL SELECTION, AND THE DIPHTHERIA VACCINE

The vaccine used to prevent diphtheria consists of the diphtheria toxoid (chemically inactivated toxin). As a consequence, when the majority of the human population in an area has been vaccinated against diphtheria, there will be a strong selective pressure against strains of *C. diphtheriae* that produce toxin. Toxin-producing strains will cause an immune response and, consequently, when they land in the throats of potential victims, they will be more rapidly eliminated from the throats of people who are vaccinated. In contrast, strains that do not produce toxin will not be as readily recognized by the immune system, and consequently will be more likely to remain circulating in the population.

In areas with high vaccine coverage, this predicted outcome has been documented. Strains of *C. diphtheriae* are found in individuals' throats, but these strains typically do not produce toxins. This type of vaccine has been considered by some to be optimal; it exerts a strong selection on bacteria to not produce the toxin but it does not completely eliminate the organisms themselves. Consequently, this type of vaccine may exert less selective pressure, favoring bacteria that produce a slightly different form of the toxin, a change that might not be effectively targeted by the current vaccine.

VACCINATION STRATEGIES

It appears that very high vaccine coverage, especially among children, is critical to prevent the development of diphtheria epidemics. In cases where an outbreak of diphtheria occurs, two strategies have been suggested. One strategy is to ensure vaccination of people who have contact with a person with diphtheria. In small outbreaks, this has been somewhat effective and has the advantage of being very cost-effective.

However, in a large-scale outbreak of diphtheria in the former Soviet Union in the 1990s, the practice of vaccinating only contacts was not effective. Only when there was widespread, high-level vaccination (>90% coverage) of the entire population, did this epidemic subside. Similarly, in an outbreak of diphtheria in 1988–1989 in China, prompt vaccination of a large proportion of the population quickly curbed the epidemic.

6

Resurgence of Diphtheria in the Former Soviet Union

In 1994, a 42-year-old Russian-born woman who had become a U.S. citizen traveled to Moscow. Within a couple of weeks, she developed a severe sore throat and fever and was hospitalized. A diagnosis of diphtheria was made, and she was treated with antitoxin and antibiotics. (It was unknown whether she had received any prior diphtheria vaccinations.) After one day in the hospital, she was transferred to another hospital in Finland, where she received additional medical treatment and where C. diphtheriae *was isolated from her throat. Ultimately, her treatment was successful, and she recovered without complications. However, she was one of more than 150,000 people who developed diphtheria in the former Soviet Union between 1990 and 1999.*[1]

EXTENT OF THE EPIDEMIC

In the Union of Soviet Socialist Republics (USSR), diphtheria had been effectively controlled by the 1970s through a combination of widespread vaccination and appropriate medical care. By 1975, there were only 198 cases in the entire USSR (out of a total population of around 250 million). However, by 1978, the incidence of diphtheria began to increase, probably due to a combination of poor follow-up to prevent the spread of diphtheria from known cases and a reduced level of vaccination and reduced potency of some of the vaccines used. The number of cases increased until

1984, when a total 1,609 cases were reported. Subsequently, there was added emphasis on identifying and treating diphtheria patients; through these efforts, by 1989 the number of cases in the USSR declined by almost half the number reported in 1984, to 839 cases.

However, a major epidemic of diphtheria erupted shortly thereafter, starting in 1990, when the number of cases increased to 1,431. The following year, the number of cases more than doubled to 3,167. At the peak of the diphtheria epidemic, in 1995, there were more than 50,000 cases. The epidemic was largely brought under control by 1999. Between 1990 and 1999, there were more than 150,000 cases and 5,000 deaths due to diphtheria. It was estimated that control measures, which were implemented starting in 1993, eventually prevented over 500,000 cases, and an additional 15,000 deaths.[2]

CAUSES OF THE EPIDEMIC

Through the 1970s, the rate of vaccination in the USSR with the standard DTP vaccine was over 90 percent. Starting in 1980, there were several changes to the vaccine and the way it was administered that helped contribute to the epidemic. One contributing factor was an alteration in the vaccination protocol, which allowed children to be vaccinated with lower-dose immunizations. This alternate vaccine had only about one-third the diphtheria toxoid that the standard vaccine had. Also, instead of four doses of vaccine, only three were recommended. This change in vaccination requirements was prompted, in part, by an exaggerated concern about the effects of DTP vaccine, especially the pertussis component. In addition, many physicians became more concerned about vaccine complications and recommended against vaccination for a number of their patients. The result was a growing population of children who were either unvaccinated or incompletely protected against diphtheria.

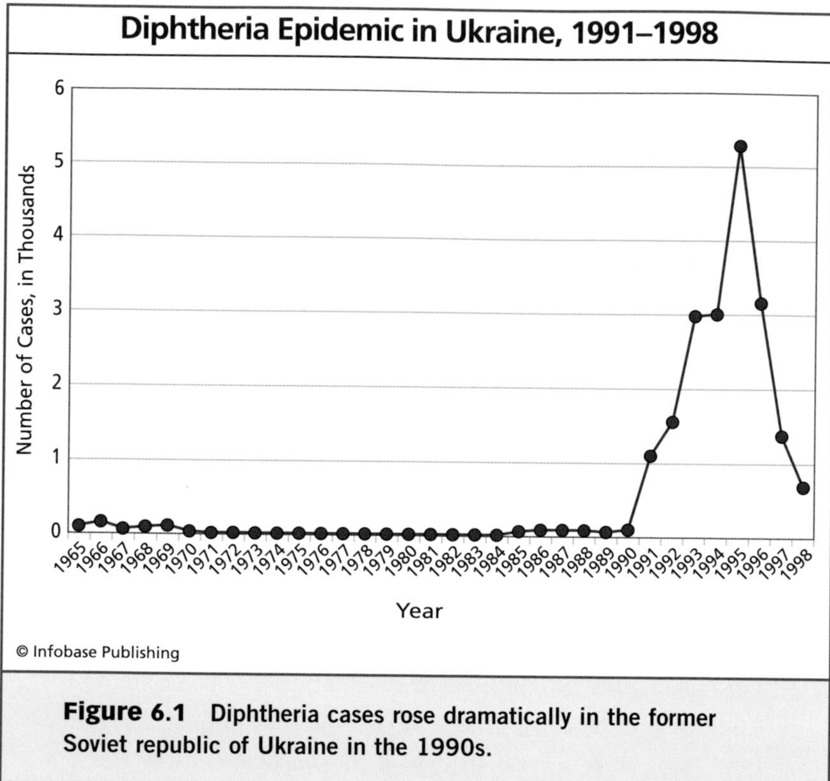

Figure 6.1 Diphtheria cases rose dramatically in the former Soviet republic of Ukraine in the 1990s.

Coupled with the reduced protection in children was a large population of adults who were unvaccinated or had not received a booster shot for so long that they were not adequately protected against diphtheria. This was particularly true of adults who were born in the 1940s and 1950s before vaccination was nearly universal throughout the USSR. In prior generations, diphtheria was so common that adults who survived into their 30s or 40s would have been exposed to diphtheria multiple times and would likely have some degree of immunity to the disease. However, as vaccination became widespread, fewer diphtheria cases developed, so many people reached adulthood with no exposure to the organism. As a result, a large population of susceptible adults was present in the population.

There were also a number of social and economic factors that contributed to the diphtheria epidemic. When the Soviet Union dissolved in 1991, there were large-scale migrations of people to and from the former Soviet republics, and with that, the spreading of diphtheria. In addition, in 1989, when the Soviet army completed its withdrawal from Afghanistan, the 100,000 troops that had been stationed there returned home. Since diphtheria is **endemic**, or constantly prevalent, in Afghanistan, some of these troops likely brought diphtheria back to their home countries.

Another factor exacerbating the diphtheria epidemic was the serious economic disruption that followed the dissolution of the Soviet Union. In many cases, the health care infrastructure deteriorated, and both vaccination to prevent diphtheria and the treatment of diphtheria was compromised.

FIGHTING THE EPIDEMIC

The initial strategy in attempting to stem the epidemic was to increase the rate of childhood diphtheria immunization and to try to ensure that the adults who had substantial contact with children (for example, teachers) were vaccinated. It quickly became clear that this strategy was not effective, since cases of diphtheria continued to increase, particularly in adults, and eventually a decision was made to vaccinate all adults.

In addition, a school-age booster immunization was reintroduced in the former Soviet republics. In 1991, less than 70 percent of children had received all their recommended vaccinations. By 1995, vaccination coverage in this age group had reached 93 percent. In addition, the number of adults who were revaccinated had also increased dramatically, with about 75 percent coverage by 1995 (as compared with about 20 percent coverage in 1990).[3]

Figure 6.2 When Soviet troops, such as the ones here, returned from fighting in Afghanistan in 1989, many of them unwittingly brought diphtheria with them. Also, the migrations and lowered vaccination rates that came after the dissolution of the USSR led to diphtheria outbreaks, particularly in Ukraine. (© Patrick Robert/ Corbis Sygma)

There was also substantial international cooperation in providing vaccines and distributing medicines. These programs were based on three main concepts:

- to provide at least one dose of vaccine to all individuals, and to provide multiple doses to the most susceptible age groups
- to quickly and appropriately treat all cases of diphtheria
- to make sure people who had contact with a person who had diphtheria received appropriate follow-up.

LESSONS LEARNED FROM THE RESURGENCE OF DIPHTHERIA

Sometimes, the benefits that have come from advances in medicine and health care can be victims of their own success. Vaccination and other medical treatments for diphtheria had been so successful that physicians and their patients in the USSR had become more concerned about the vaccine itself. This created lapses in vaccinations, which provided a fertile ground for infection in unvaccinated and inadequately vaccinated individuals.

One of the lessons from this epidemic is that societies cannot be complacent in their battles with infectious diseases. For most infections, humans have reached, at best, an uneasy truce but not a complete victory. A breakdown in the health care system can quickly lead to a resurgence in cases of a variety of infectious diseases.

Another lesson from this epidemic is that humans are increasingly connected to one another. As travel becomes easier and faster, the potential for the transmission of disease from areas where it is common to areas where it is rare becomes more and more likely.

A third lesson is that preventing an epidemic is typically much more cost-effective than trying to control it once it has exploded. The cost in dollars, deaths, and pain and suffering when an epidemic occurs is considerable, particularly in comparison with the relatively small cost of vaccination and other public health measures to prevent the spread of disease.

In particular, programs that target the vaccination of more than 90 percent of infants (starting at the age of two months) and include boosters for school-age children and adults, are a critical component of successfully preventing diphtheria epidemics. This, combined with a monitoring program to ensure proper vaccine coverage and treatment of diphtheria cases, should reduce the risk of epidemics in the future.

7

Uses of Diphtheria Toxin

A 24-year-old woman visited her physician for a skin condition that had persisted for two years. She had a number of bumps under the skin on her arm, thighs, and back. These bumps developed at about the same time that she started to have joint pain and a fever. Initially, she was treated with steroids and other drugs with little success. On a subsequent examination, laboratory tests showed that the bumps under her skin were concentrations of lymphomas, a type of cancer involving the immune system. She was therefore treated with an anticancer drug that contained diphtheria toxin. The drug was intended to target the cancer cells, and the diphtheria toxin would then kill the cells. The therapy was successful, and she showed no signs of the cancer nine months after treatment.[1]

In an interesting twist, diphtheria toxin is now being used to treat some other diseases, and it has also found use as a tool in fundamental studies in biology. As scientists have gained a greater understanding of how the toxin works, they have become able to harness the toxin to kill certain types of cancer cells. They have also developed techniques for using diphtheria toxin to precisely destroy specific types of cells in experimental animals.

CANCER TREATMENT

The potential for diphtheria toxin to be a useful treatment for cancer was suggested at least as early as 1974. Researchers at the University of Oregon Medical School reported that some tumor cells from mice and humans were up to 10,000 times more sensitive to diphtheria toxin, compared to normal cells. This initial observation was subsequently exploited to develop therapeutically useful cancer drugs.[2]

Cancer is the uncontrolled growth of cells in the body. Normally, the multiplication of cells in our bodies is tightly regulated; disruption of that regulation often involves some change in the surface of the cancerous cell that differentiates it from normal cells. While this difference helps the cancer cell grow and divide, it also provides a target that has been exploited as the basis for several new strategies for treating cancer.

One example of a drug that targets and destroys cancer cells based on unique features of the surface of the cells is called denileukin diftitox (trade name Ontak®). This drug was approved by the U.S. Food and Drug Administration for the treatment of **lymphomas** (cancers of the lymph nodes) that have not responded to other treatments.

Denileukin diftitox is made in the bacterium *Escherichia coli* using recombinant DNA technology and then extensively purified. This drug is a hybrid of two proteins including a portion of the diphtheria toxin. As described previously, the diphtheria toxin consists of three sections, each of which has a unique function. One section (designated "A") is the active portion, which actually does the damage inside the cell. A second section (designated "T") allows the toxin to enter the cytoplasm, the cellular material of the cell. The third section (denoted with a "B") is the binding portion, which allows the toxin to latch onto the surface of cells with the appropriate surface molecules. In denileukin diftitox, the binding portion of the diphtheria toxin is replaced with the binding portion of the interleukin-2 molecule. Interleukin 2 is a small protein that is involved in transmitting signals to cells. It sends these signals by binding to an interleukin-2 receptor on the surface of the cells. So instead of binding to cells that are the normal target of diphtheria toxin, this drug binds to cells that express the interleukin-2 receptor.

The interleukin-2 receptor is found at high levels on the surface of some lymphoma cells, and this receptor transmits signals that help those cells grow in an uncontrolled manner.

The section of the drug containing the interleukin-2 protein will home in on these cancer cells. Once attached to the cell, the interaction of the drug with the receptor causes this agent to be pulled into the cell, in a little bag surrounded by a portion of the cell membrane. At this point, the remaining portion of the drug, which contains the diphtheria toxin, goes into action. The cell makes that little bag that contains the drug acidic, and this changes the shape of the toxin. The toxin inserts itself into the membrane, and the active portion of the

WHY USE DIPHTHERIA TOXIN TO KILL CELLS?

A number of strategies have been developed to destroy tumors and other cells. These include the use of antibodies, which target certain cells and lead to cell–antibody combination being eliminated by the immune system. Another alternative is to attach a radioactive molecule to an antibody. Once attached to a cell, the radioactivity damages and possibly destroys the targeted cell.

In comparison to these other methods, an advantage of using diphtheria toxin is that it is extremely potent. A single molecule of the toxin is sufficient to kill a cell, so one can be more assured that a targeted cell is actually being destroyed.[3]

In cases where the goal is to destroy certain types of cells to better understand the function of those cells, the system used involves incorporating the diphtheria toxin into the genome of an organism. This means that animals that are normally fairly resistant to diphtheria toxin because the toxin cannot readily enter their cells (for example, mice) are still susceptible to diphtheria toxin generated within their cells. Consequently, this system can be used to study cells and tissues in a variety of animals.

toxin is ejected into the cytoplasm. Then the toxin homes in on the protein-making machinery in the cell. The toxin effectively stops this process, and since protein production is required for the survival of cancer cells, these dangerous cells are destroyed. In the first small clinical trials of patients with cutaneous T-cell lymphoma, reported in 2001 and 2003, 30 percent to 60 percent had a positive response to treatment, with a small number having a complete remission of symptoms.[4]

As with most cancer treatments, there are both limitations and side effects. Only about 60 percent of the cancer cells targeted by this therapy (cutaneous T-cell lymphoma) have the interleukin-2 receptor on their surface. In addition, several key cell types in the immune system (T-cells, B-cells, and natural killer cells) have the interleukin-2 receptor on their surface, meaning this treatment will kill those cells as well. Consequently, like other cancer drugs, this treatment can have a number of harmful side effects. In trials to date, the most severe effects have been acute allergic reactions and leakage of fluid from the blood vessels. Another potential problem with this therapy is immunity to diphtheria toxin by virtue of having been vaccinated with DTaP, Tdap, or Td. In one clinical trial, prior to treatment nearly half of the patients tested had a preexisting immune response, which reduced the effectiveness of the drug. After three cycles of treatment, nearly all patients had an immune response against the drug, which likely impaired its activity.[5]

This drug has been used in clinical trials for several other cancer cell types (for example, non-Hodgkin's lymphoma and non–small cell lung cancer). In some cases, these treatments have resulted in complete or partial remission, indicating a potential role for this drug in treating at least a subgroup of patients with these diseases.

A modification of this strategy has also been found to be useful in treating acute myeloid leukemia (AML), the most common acute form of **leukemia** (cancer involving white blood cells) in the United States. Although many therapies have been

Figure 7.1 Chemotherapy drugs, such as those shown here, are sometimes created using bacteria or the toxins they produce. The chemotherapy drug denileukin diftitox is made in the *Escherichia coli* bacterium and contains diphtheria toxin. (Bill Branson/ National Cancer Institute/U.S. National Institutes of Health)

developed to treat this illness, upward of one-third of cases relapse. These relapsed cases are very difficult to treat, and the survival rate is very low (almost no patients are still alive at two years). An experimental therapy was developed to treat cases of relapsed AML. It included a "homing" protein specific to this type of cancer, attached to the same active portion of the diphtheria toxin used in denileukin diftitox. The "homing" protein specifically attaches to the cancer cells, bringing the diphtheria toxin with it. Once attached, the diphtheria toxin is pulled into the cells, which are then killed by the toxin. This treatment has helped some people with relapsed and otherwise untreatable disease. For example, one 33-year-old woman had been treated for AML and, after about a year, her cancer relapsed. Following treatment with the diphtheria toxin and "homing" protein, she had another remission and survived for a year, much longer than the typical weeks or months for this type of relapsed cancer.[6]

Another potential use of denileukin diftitox in cancer therapy is as an initial treatment prior to the infusion of a cancer vaccine. One trial showed that the vaccine worked better after the use of denileukin diftitox, presumably because this drug destroyed immune cells that were otherwise preventing a response to the vaccine.[7]

There have been a number of other experiments where diphtheria toxin was used to destroy other types of tumors. For example, research has been conducted to determine if a virus containing diphtheria toxin could specifically target prostate tumors. Although the experiments were only performed on cells in culture and in mice, the virus worked well, which suggests that this strategy may be an important step in developing a therapy for prostate cancer.[8]

OTHER APPLICATIONS OF TOXIN

Another potential use for the diphtheria toxin gene would be to destroy HIV-infected cells. In this case a virus is constructed that will infect cells that contain HIV. This virus contains the diphtheria toxin gene under the control of a DNA sequence that requires HIV proteins for activation. Therefore, diphtheria toxin will be produced only in cells that are infected with HIV and will destroy only those infected cells.[9]

Developing a mechanism for destroying HIV-infected cells has become a priority with the availability of highly active antiretroviral therapy, which can reduce virus concentrations in the blood to levels below the limits of detection. Since HIV can remain hidden and inactive in some cells, a strategy for homing in on these cells and destroying them could be a strategy that, combined with other treatments, might conceivably lead to the eradication of HIV from the body.

UNDERSTANDING BASIC BIOLOGY

Fighting cancer using diphtheria toxin relies on the ability of this potent toxin to quickly kill cells once the toxin gets inside. In a similar vein, diphtheria toxin has been useful in helping to understand the function of various tissues in a variety of organisms.

One common method for trying to understand the importance of a group of cells or tissues is to destroy them and determine what happens to the organisms. Diphtheria

OTHER USES OF DIPHTHERIA TOXIN

The diseases that have been targeted by denileukin diftitox are those that involve cells that have high levels of interleukin-2 receptors on their surfaces. As experience with this drug has grown, other conditions that involve these types of cells have become potential targets for this therapy.

Denileukin diftitox has been used in clinical trials in cases of transplant rejection that could not be treated by other means. Transplant rejection, in part, involves cells of the immune system that carry the interleukin-2 receptor on their surface. Treatment with this drug will destroy those cells, thus potentially reducing the risk of rejection. In one small study, 71 percent of patients experiencing severe transplant rejection showed a positive response to this therapy.[10]

Another condition for which denileukin diftitox has been tested is psoriasis. This is a skin condition that results in red, scaly, painful patches of skin. One contributing factor to psoriasis is overactivity of immune system cells that contain the interleukin-2 receptor, making denileukin diftitox treatment potentially useful. In one study, 7 of 15 patients showed significant improvement following treatment, and it is likely this drug will be tested in additional clinical studies with psoriasis patients.[11]

toxin, along with other toxins, has been used to destroy certain cells or tissues. The trick is targeting these cells and tissues in a way that does not kill the organism. In these experiments, the diphtheria toxin gene is inserted into the genome of the organism, a molecular version of a ticking time bomb. A variety of genetic tricks have then been used to get the "bomb" to go off at the right time and in the right place.

This technique of specifically destroying specific cells or tissues using controlled expression of diphtheria toxin has

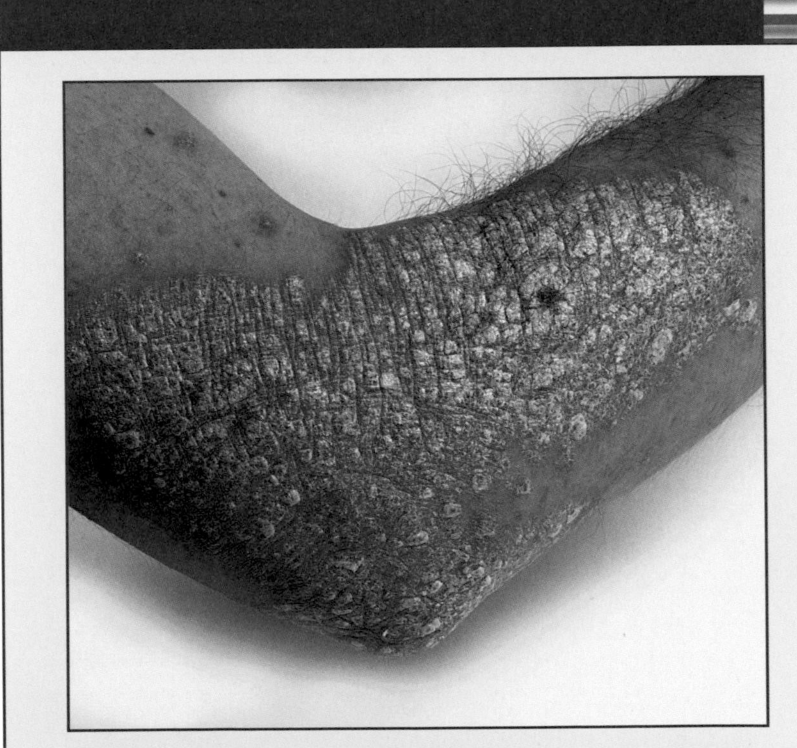

Figure 7.2 Psoriasis, shown here on an arm, causes a scaly, painful rash. Denileukin diftitox, a drug that contains diphtheria toxin, may prove useful in the treatment of this condition. (© Kenxro/ShutterStock Images)

been widely used. Several strategies for limiting toxin expression to particular cells or tissues have been tested. One of the most common is a system called Cre-Lox. It involves using a gene of interest (like the diphtheria toxin gene) that is inactive because it has a section of another DNA inserted in the middle of it. The inserted DNA is located between two DNA sequences called Lox sites. Another gene, called Cre, is placed under the control of a section of DNA that is active only in certain cell types. Consequently, the Cre protein is produced only in those specific cell types. By placing the Cre gene under the control of different sections of DNA in different strains of mice or other experimental animals, Cre can specifically be produced in a variety of different tissues. When the Cre gene is activated, it recognizes the Lox sites and removes the inserted DNA from the diphtheria toxin gene so that the toxin is now produced only in cells with an active Cre gene.

This system has been used for a variety of purposes, primarily in mice. For example, experiments demonstrated the usefulness of this system to prevent the formation of sperm cells, to detect which genes affect the function of the liver, to determine which genes affect the formation of cells of the immune system, and to determine how fat tissue regulates obesity. In the latter example, researchers designed a genetic system where the diphtheria toxin was expressed only in fat cells. Different strains of mice were generated, each of which produced different amounts of diphtheria toxin in the fat tissue. Mice whose cells produced enough toxin to kill all fat cells in the body died shortly after birth. Mice with a lower level of toxin expression started losing fat at about four months and were obesity-resistant.[12] In another example, researchers wanted to determine the effect of eliminating brown fat from animals, using expression of the diphtheria toxin under the control of a section of DNA active only in brown fat. These animals were obesity-resistant but were sensitive to the cold.[13]

8

Future Prospects Regarding Diphtheria

Considering the fact that sharp winds, gasses given off from decaying animals, and living in low-lying areas were thought to be contributing or causative factors for diphtheria in the mid-1800s, the knowledge that has developed over the past 150 years or so has led to tremendous advances culminating in the almost complete disappearance of diphtheria in many countries.

However, in many parts of the world, diphtheria is still a threat, as shown in Table 8.1. In many countries, the health care infrastructure for eradicating the disease does not yet exist. Consequently, there is still a good deal of work to be done to control this serious infection.

NEW DEVELOPMENTS IN DIAGNOSIS

The ability to identify individuals who have diphtheria quickly continues to be an important tool in limiting the spread of disease. As described previously, molecular methods are being introduced that can rapidly identify *C. diphtheriae* based on unique gene sequences in that organism.

As an extension of that strategy, new methods are also being developed to try to trace the spread of the organism from person to person. A key to this methodology is to determine if the same strain of *C. diphtheriae* has infected a number of people. If so, it might give clues to how the bacteria are being transmitted from person to person and allow a plan to be developed to block transmission.

For example, in response to the epidemic of diphtheria in the former Soviet Union during the 1990s, researchers at the St. Petersburg Pasteur Institute in Russia developed a method for identifying *C. diphtheriae* strains by using DNA sequences that vary significantly even between closely related strains. This technique is similar to one developed for studying *Mycobacterium tuberculosis* strains, and it may be useful in understanding how bacteria are transmitted during future epidemics of diphtheria.[1]

NEW DEVELOPMENTS IN VACCINATION

Diphtheria toxoid vaccination is both highly effective and very safe. However, there has been an interest in trying to develop a vaccine that is even more effective and causes fewer side effects. One example of work toward this goal was the development of the DTaP vaccine; this vaccine has substantially reduced the incidence of side effects compared to the older version of this immunization.

In terms of enhancing vaccine effectiveness, researchers at the University of Oregon Health Sciences Center showed in 1976 that there are differences in the antibodies that are produced (at

Table 8.1 Countries Where Diphtheria Circulates in the Population

Africa	Algeria, Angola, Egypt, Niger, Nigeria, Sudan, and sub-Saharan countries
Americas	Bolivia, Brazil, Colombia, Dominican Republic, Ecuador, Haiti, and Paraguay
Asia/South Pacific	Afghanistan, Bangladesh, Bhutan, Burma (Myanmar), Cambodia, China, India, Indonesia, Laos, Malaysia, Mongolia, Nepal, Pakistan, Papua New Guinea, Philippines, Thailand, and Vietnam
Middle East	Iran, Iraq, Saudi Arabia, Syria, Turkey, and Yemen
Europe	Albania, Russia, and countries of the former Soviet Union

Source: CDC[2]

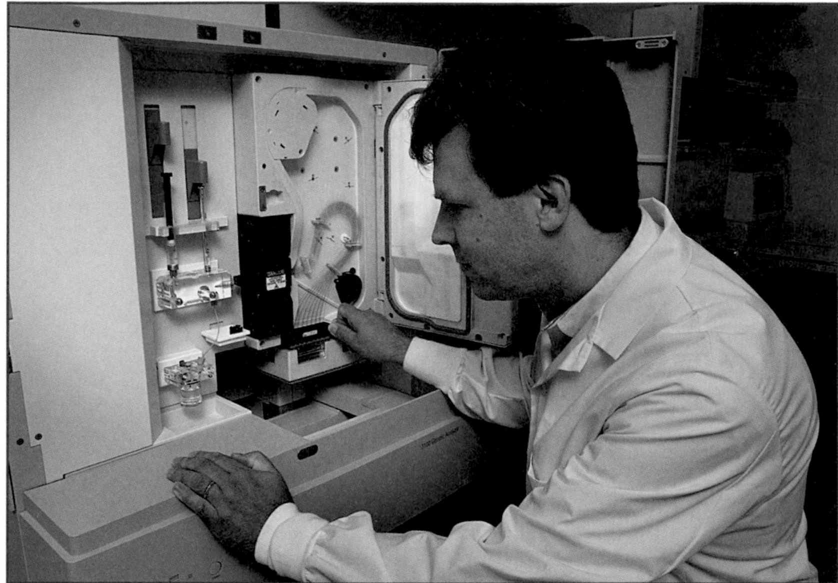

Figure 8.1 The laboratories of the Centers for Disease Control and Prevention (CDC), shown here, have conducted DNA sequencing to differentiate *C. diphtheriae* strains. This may prove useful in further understanding the disease. (CDC/Maryam I. Daneshvar, Ph.D.)

least in mice) in response to diphtheria toxin, compared to the diphtheria toxoid found in the vaccine. Although antibodies to the toxin and toxoid had similar abilities to neutralize toxin, it is possible that the use of a more natural toxin could induce a more protective response in at least some people.[3]

In addition, at least in a theoretical sense, it would be safer if the starting material for producing the toxoid was a toxin that had already been disarmed. For example, a change in one or two amino acids in the toxin can render it completely harmless, yet the disabled toxin would still be able to induce an immune response. Recent attempts to develop safer and more effective vaccines have primarily focused on **recombinant DNA** techniques to modify the diphtheria toxin. For example, work by a group of researchers in France involved creating a protein that combined portions of the diphtheria toxin gene with another bacterial gene (the other gene made the recombinant protein easier to purify and potentially more likely to be recognized by the immune system). The resulting protein was tested both with cells growing in laboratory culture and in rabbits. Although the resulting protein did not lead to as great an immune response as the toxoid currently used in the vaccine, it did cause a detectable immune response and might be a starting point for the development of newer vaccine.[4]

Another goal in vaccine improvement is to reduce the number of immunizations required to produce immunity, with the aim of ultimately producing a vaccine that requires only a single dose to confer lifelong protection. One strategy that tends to produce longer-lasting immunity is the use of a live, weakened pathogen in the vaccine. This organism typically reproduces to a limited extent in the body, and the result is a much more vigorous immune response, which results in longer-lasting immunity.

If this strategy were to be used for diphtheria vaccination, it would be critical that the live organism in the vaccine produced a non-harmful, mutant version of the toxin. Extensive work by biochemists and geneticists has identified a number of amino acids in the toxin that are critical for its function. These can be readily altered using genetic engineering techniques to produce mutant toxin that is inactive. However, researchers at Harvard University showed that, in some cases, a second mutation could restore some of the toxin's function. Since mutation can occur naturally in a living microbe, this suggests that any recombinant toxin designed for use in a living vaccine will have to be engineered carefully to ensure that it cannot mutate into a functional form.[5]

NEW DEVELOPMENTS IN TREATMENTS

Currently, the only treatment available to inactivate the diphtheria toxin circulating in the body is the use of antitoxin prepared in horses. Although this antitoxin is highly effective for most patients, for some—particularly those allergic to horse serum—it requires testing and desensitization; in cases of severe allergy, it may not be usable at all.

Consequently, there has been interest in looking at alternative strategies for preventing circulating diphtheria toxin from entering and destroying cells. One strategy that has been considered is the purification of antitoxin from humans who had recovered from diphtheria, received a recent diphtheria vaccination, or both. In one paper published in 2004, researchers from Russia and the Netherlands determined that many patients who had recovered from diphtheria had high levels of antibodies in their bloodstreams and thus could be potential donors of antitoxin to treat the disease in others. The use of serum from human donors who are immune to diphtheria could result in fewer side effects, compared to using horse serum, and may become an option for treating patients in the future.[6]

Another possible alternative was developed by a group of scientists at the University of Texas Southwestern Medical Center at Dallas and reported in a 2002 paper. This group identified a molecule on the surface of cells that acts as a receptor for the toxin; it binds to diphtheria toxin and causes it to be internalized. They reasoned that if a soluble form of the toxin receptor was injected into people who had diphtheria, this form of the growth factor would act like a sponge and sop up the diphtheria toxin before it could enter cells and cause damage. In their work, the researchers developed a genetically engineered version of the protein that bound diphtheria toxin more tightly but had fewer effects on human cells, compared to the natural receptor. The natural receptor is called heparin-binding epidermal growth factor-like growth factor. The initial tests indicated that the engineered version of this molecule could prevent diphtheria toxin from binding to sensitive cells grown in culture dishes.[7] Other improvements in treatment may occur as we gain a better understanding of the biology of this microbe and the strategies it uses to cause disease.

SEQUENCING THE COMPLETE GENOME

In 2003, the complete genome sequence of a strain of *C. diphtheriae* involved in the epidemic in the former Soviet Union was published. This was an important step because previously, relatively little was known about the genetics of this pathogen. The genome contains all the genetic instructions of an organism. For this microbe, the genome contains approximately 2.5 million **base pairs**. (A base pair is the smallest subunit of DNA—it is a single instruction in the genetic code.) This is about 1,000 times smaller than the human genome, but the sequencing was still a considerable undertaking, involving at least 26 scientists.[8] The sequence provides a starting point to understanding the function of all the genes present in the organism. These genes provide the blueprint for all the various features *C. diphtheriae* has that allow it to be such a successful pathogen. Consequently, scientists now have the tools to substantially advance our understanding of this pathogen and how it causes disease.

The genome sequence identified a number of genes for **fimbriae**, small hair-like projections from the cell that are often involved in binding to human cells. Also identified in *C. diphtheriae* were a series of genes involved in iron uptake and other genes that play a role in the export of proteins. The genome sequence also provided an opportunity to analyze how some critical virulence genes may be regulated. For example, researchers in India, basing their studies on a computer analysis of the genome sequence, suggested that the gene that regulates the production of diphtheria toxin also plays a role in responding to stress caused by excessive iron in the cell. This type of analysis would not have been possible without the availability of the genome sequence.[9] In addition, some of these recently identified genes may be useful targets for interventions in helping to treat disease by targeting genes or processes unique to this microbe.

OTHER DEVELOPMENTS IN GENETICS

There have also been some improvements in the techniques for studying the genes in this organism. Commonly, geneticists study an organism by destroying the function of a gene and determining the result. Until recently, the methods for doing this in *C. diphtheriae* were cumbersome and not always successful. A 2002 report by scientists at the University of Colorado Health Science Center described a method for making mutations that should help clarify the role of some of the genes identified through the genome sequence. In this method, a **mobile genetic element** (sometimes called a "jumping gene") randomly inserts into the genome of the organism. Typically, when these elements insert, they inactivate the gene where they land. It is relatively easy to determine the insertion site of the mobile element and, therefore, the mutated gene. Using this technique, it was possible to generate mutations in the gene that regulates the production of diphtheria toxin. As with the genome sequence, this genetic technique is likely to provide a better understanding of the virulence factors present in this organism, and it could lead to improved methods of treating and preventing diphtheria.[10]

THE FUTURE

Diphtheria is one of the most striking examples of a disease where the identification of the pathogen, and an understanding of the disease process, quickly led to effective treatments and a vaccine that could prevent disease. Yet in spite of these medical advances, there is still a great deal that we do not understand about this organism and how it causes disease. Modern advances in biomedical science continue to pull back the curtains to these mysteries. For example, the availability of the genome sequence of *C. diphtheriae* should allow us to develop a much more complete understanding of the biology of this pathogen.

Yet in spite of all that is known about diphtheria, continued vigilance is important. There have been several examples where complacency led to outbreaks that sickened and killed many people, such as the epidemic in the former Soviet Union during the 1990s. Hopefully, a better understanding of this disease will make us more vigilant and will allow people to remain free of the scourge of diphtheria for generations to come.

Notes

Chapter 1

1. P. Lurie, H. Stafford, P. Tran, C. Teacher, R. Ankeny, M. Barron, J. Bart, K. Bisgard, T. Tiwari, T. Murphy, J. Moran, and P. Cassiday, "Fatal Respiratory Diphtheria in a U.S. Traveler to Haiti—Pennsylvania, 2003," *Morbidity and Mortality Weekly Report* 52, 53 (2004): 1285–1286.
2. W. Atkinson, J. Hamborsky, L. McIntyre, and S. Wolfe, eds. "Diphtheria" in *Epidemiology and Prevention of Vaccine-Preventable Diseases* (Washington: Public Health Foundation, 2007) 59–70.
3. P. English, "Diphtheria and Theories of Infectious Disease: Centennial Appreciation of the Critical Role of Diphtheria in the History of Medicine," *Pediatrics* 76 (1985): 1–9.
4. H. Hoffman and M. Frank, "Time-Lapse Photomicrography of Lashing, Flexing, and Snapping Movements in *Escherichia coli* and *Corynebacterium* Microcultures," *Journal of Bacteriology* 90, 3 (1965): 789–795.
5. M.B.D. Coyle, J. Nowowiejski, J. Q. Russell, and N. B. Groman, "Laboratory Review of Reference Strains of *Corynebacterium diphtheriae* Indicates Mistyped Intermedius Strains," *Journal of Clinical Microbiology* 31, 11 (Nov. 1993): 3060–3062.
6. T. Hadfield, P. McEvoy, Y. Polotsky, V. A. Tzinserling, and A. A. Yakovlev, "The Pathology of Diphtheria," *The Journal of Infectious Diseases* 181, Suppl. 1 (2000): S116–120.
7. R. MacGregor, "*Corynebacterium diphtheriae*," in *Principles and Practices of Infectious Diseases*, 4th ed, (New York: Churchill Livingstone, 1995): 1865–1872.
8. Centers for Disease Control and Prevention, "Diphtheria," http://www.cdc.gov/vaccines/pubs/pinkbook/downloads/dip.pdf, accessed March 23, 2008.
9. J. Chin, ed., *Control of communicable Diseases in Man*, 17th ed. (Washington: American Public Health Association, 2000).
10. E. Jones, R. Kim-Farley, M. Algunaid, M. Parvez, Y. Ballad, A. Hightower, W, Orenstein, and C. Broome, "Diphtheria: A Possible Foodborne Outbreak in Hodeida, Yemen Arab Republic," *Bulletin of the World Health Organization* 63, 2 (1985): 287–293.
11. A. M. Fraser, "A Case of Diphtheria in a Horse," *Public Health* 21 (1908): 48–49.
12. F. Renom, M. Garau, M. Rubı, F. Ramis, A. Galmes, and J. B. Soriano, "Nosocomial Outbreak of *Corynebacterium striatum* Infection in Patients with Chronic Obstructive Pulmonary Disease," *Journal of Clinical Microbiology* 45, 6 (June 2007): 2064–2067.
13. A. Zoysa, P. Hawkey, K. Engler, R. George, G. Mann, W. Reilly, D. Taylor, and A. Efstratiou, "Characterization of Oxygenic *Corynebacterium ulcerans* Strains Isolated from Humans and Domestic Cats in the United Kingdom," *Journal of Clinical Microbiology* 43, 9 (2005): 4377–4381.

Chapter 2

1. P. English, "Diphtheria and Theories of Infectious Disease: Centennial Appreciation of the Critical Role of Diphtheria in the History of Medicine," *Pediatrics* 76 (1985): 1–9.
2. Heritage Language Technologies, "Of Aretæus, the Cappadocian. Causes and Symptoms of Acute Disease," Digital Hippocrates, *Book I, Chapter IX*, http://www.chlt.org/sandbox/dh/aretaeusEnglish/page.12.a.php?size=240x320, accessed September 2, 2008.
3. M. MacKenzie, *Diphtheria; its nature and treatment.* (Philadelphia: Lindsay and Blackiston, 1879).
4. A. Galzaka and S. Robertson, *Diphtheria*, World Health Organization, 1996, http://whqlibdoc.who.int/publications/2004/9241592303_chap3.pdf, accessed March 23, 2008.

5. C. Neidhard, *Diphtheria, as It Prevailed in the United States, 1860–1866*, (New York: William Radde, 1867).
6. E. Klebs, "Umber Diphtheria," *Vern. D. Congresses f. Inn. Med., II. Congr. Bergmann Weisbaden* (1883), 139–154.
7. H. Lechevailier and M. Solotorovsky, *Three Centuries of Microbiology*, (New York: McGraw-Hill Book Company, 1965).
8. G. Nutgall and G. Graham-Smith, eds. *The Bacteriology of diphtheria.* (Cambridge Mass: Cambridge University Press, 1908).
9. T. Brock, *Milestones of Microbiology*, (Washington: ASM Press, 1999).
10. A. Silverstein, *Paul Ehrlich's Receptor Immunology, The Magnificent Obsession* (San Diego: Academic Press, 2002).
11. From *Nobel Lectures, Physiology or Medicine 1901–1921.* Elsevier Publishing Company, Amsterdam, 1967, http://nobelprize.org/nobel_prizes/medicine/laureates/1908/ehrlich-bio.html, accessed April 11, 2008.
12 E. Hammonds, *Childhood's Deadly Scourge. The Campaign to Control Diphtheria in New York City 1880–1930* (Baltimore: Johns Hopkins University Press, 1999).
13. W. Park and A. Zingher, "Diphtheria immunity: natural, active, and passive. Its determination by the Schick test," *American Journal for Public Health* 6, 5 (1916): 431–445
14. C. Vitek, "Diphtheria," *Current Topics in Microbiology and Immunology* 304 (2006): 71–94.
15. Calculations based on: Average salary, 2006, approximately 55,000 Euros/year in Germany; Average salary, 1900, approximately 1,200 marks per year. Exchange rate (as of February 2008) of $1.47 dollars per Euro. http://www.germannotes.com/hist_mark.shtml; http://www.destatis.de/jetspeed/portal/cms/Sites/destatis/Internet/EN/Navigation/Statistics/VerdiensteArbeitskosten/Bruttoverdienste/Bruttoverdienste.psml, accessed February 2008.
16. Food and Drug Administration, *Biologics Centennial: 100 years of Biologics Regulation*, http://www.fda.gov/oc/history/makinghistory/100yearsofbiologics.html, accessed April 11, 2008.
17. I. Ebiswa, "The encounter of Gaston Ramon (1886–1963) with formalin: A biographical study of a great scientist," *Kitasato Archives of Experimental Medicine* 60, 3 (1987): 55–70.
18. P. English, "Diphtheria and Theories of Infectious Disease: Centennial Appreciation of the Critical Role of Diphtheria in the History of Medicine," *Pediatrics* 76 (1985): 1–9.
19. C. Neidhard, *Diphtheria, as it Prevailed in the United States, 1860–1866*, (New York: William Radde, 1867).
20. World Health Organization. *Diphtheria.* http://www.who.int/immunization_monitoring/diseases/diphteria/en/index.html, accessed April 11, 2008.
21. C. Vitek, "Diphtheria," *Current Topics in Microbiology and Immunology* 304 (2006): 71–94.

Chapter 3

1. L. Robison, F, Rahaman, and I. Zamiri, "Diphtheria in an elderly woman: unexpected sequelae," *Journal of the Royal Society of Medicine* 80, (1987): 584–585.
2. R. Collier, "Effect of diphtheria toxin on protein synthesis: Inactivation of one of the transfer factors," *Journal of Molecular Biology* 25 (1967): 83–98.
3. V. Freeman, "Studies on the virulence of bacteriophage-infected strains of *Corynebacterium diphtheriae*," *The Journal of Bacteriology* 61 (1951): 675–688.
4. W. L. Barksdale and A. M. Pappenheimer, "Phage-host relationships in nontoxigenic and toxigenic diphtheria bacilli," *Journal of Bacteriology* 60, (1954): 220–231.
5. Y. Li, J. McCadden, F. Ferrer, M. Kruszewski, M. Carducci, J. Simons, and R. Rodriguez, "Prostate-specific Expression of the Diphtheria Toxin A

Chain (DT-A): Studies of Inducibility and Specificity of Expression of Prostate-specific Antigen Promoter-driven DT-A Adenoviral-mediated Gene Transfer," *Cancer Research* 62 (2002): 2576–2582.
6. R. Collier, "Understanding the mode of action of diphtheria toxin: a perspective on progress during the 20th Century," *Toxicon* 39 (2001): 1793–1803.
7. D. Marra Oram, A. Jacobson, and R. Holmes, "Transcription of the Contiguous sigB, dtxR, and galE Genes in *Corynebacterium diphtheriae*: Evidence for Multiple Transcripts and Regulation by Environmental Factors," *Journal of Bacteriology* 188, 8 (2006): 2959–2973.
8. S. Yellaboina, S. Ranjan, P. Chakhaiyar, S. Hasnain, and A. Ranjan, "Prediction of DtxR regulon: Identification of binding sites and operons controlled by Diphtheria toxin repressor in *Corynebacterium diphtheriae*," *BioMed Central Microbiology* 4 (2004): 38.
9. D. Marra Oram, A. Avdalovic, and R. K. Holmes, "Construction and Characterization of Transposon Insertion Mutations in *Corynebacterium diphtheriae* That Affect Expression of the Diphtheria Toxin Repressor (DtxR)," *Journal of Bacteriology* 184, 20 (2002): 5723–5732.
10. A. M. Cerdeno-Tarraga et al. "The complete genome sequence and analysis of *Corynebacterium diphtheriae* NCTC13129," *Nucleic Acids Research* 31, 2 (2003): 6516–6523.

Chapter 4

1. I. Shah, "Diphtheria," *Pediatric oncall*, http://www.pediatriconcall.com/fordoctor/casereports/diphtheria.asp, accessed July 15, 2008.
2. R. MacGregor, *"Corynebacterium diphtheriae,"* in *Principles and Practices of Infectious Diseases,* 4th Ed, (New York: Churchill Livingstone, 1995): 1865–1872.
3. K. Enger, and A. Efstratiou, "Rapid enzyme immunoassay for determination of toxigenicty among clinical isolates of Corynebacteria," *Journal of Clinical Microbiology* 38, 4 (2000): 1385–1389.
4. A. Efstratiou, K. Engler, C. Dawes, and D. Sesardic, "Comparison of Phenotypic and Genotypic Methods for Detection of Diphtheria Toxin among Isolates of Pathogenic Corynebacteria," *Journal of Clinical Microbiology* 36, 11 (1998): 3173–3177.
5. T. Komiya, N. Shibata, M. Ito, M. Takahashi, and Y. Arakawa, "Retrospective diagnosis of diphtheria by detection of the *Corynebacterium diphtheriae* tox gene in a formaldehyde-fixed throat swab using PCR and sequencing analysis," *Journal of Clinical Microbiology* 38, 6 (2000): 2400–2402.
6. R. J. Collier, "Diphtheria toxin: Mode of action and structure," *Bacteriological Reviews* 39, 1 (1975): 54–85.
7. G. Nutall and G. Graham-Smith, eds. *The Bacteriology of diphtheria.* (Cambridge, Mass: Cambridge University Press, 1908).
8. R. MacGregor, "*Corynebacterium diphtheriae*," in *Principles and Practices of Infectious Diseases,* 4th ed., G. Mandell, J. Bennett, and R. Dolin, eds, (New York: Churchill Livingstone, 1995) 1865–1872.
9. G. Nutgall and G. Graham-Smith, eds. *The Bacteriology of Diphtheria.* (Cambridge Mass: Cambridge University Press, 1908).
10. W. Jenner, *Diphtheria, Its Symptoms and Treatment,* (London: Walton and Maberly, 1861).
11. M. MacKenzie, *Diphtheria; its nature and Treatment.* (Philadelphia: Lindsay and Blackiston, 1879),

Chapter 5

1. C. Hardman. "A death from diphtheria," *Immunization Action Coalition*, http://www.immunize.org/reports/report026.pdf, accessed April 15, 2008.
2. Centers for Disease Control and Prevention, "Pertussis Vaccination: Use of Acellular Pertussis Vaccines Among Infants and Young Children

Recommendations of the Advisory Committee on Immunization Practices (ACIP)," *Morbidity and Mortality Weekly Report* 46, RR-7 (1997): 1–25.

3. Centers for Disease Control and Prevention, "2008 Childhood and Adolescent Immunization Schedule," *Centers for Disease Control,* http://www.cdc.gov/nip/recs/child-schedule.htm#Printable, accessed April 3, 2008.
4. B. Song and R. Katial, "Update on Side Effects from Common Vaccines," *Current Allergy and Asthma Reports* 4 (2004): 447–453.
5. Centers for Disease Control and Prevention, "Diphtheria, Pertussis, and Tetanus Vaccines. What You Need to Know," http://www.cdc.gov/vaccines/pubs/vis/downloads/vis-dtap.pdf, accessed March 31, 2008.
6. Centers for Disease Control and Prevention, "Diphtheria, Pertussis, and Tetanus Vaccines. What you need to know," http://www.cdc.gov/vaccines/pubs/vis/downloads/vis-dtap.pdf, accessed March 31, 2008.
7. J. Lloyd, P. Haber, G. Mootrey, M. Braun, P. Rhodes, and R. Chen, VAERS Working Group, "Adverse event reporting rates following tetanus-diphtheria and tetanus toxoid vaccinations: data from the Vaccine Adverse Event Reporting System (VAERS), 1991–1997," *Vaccine* 21 (2003): 3746–3750.
8. S. Rosenthal and R.T. Chen, "The reporting sensitivities of two passive surveillance systems for vaccine adverse events," *American Journal of Public Health* 85, 12 (1995): 1706–1709.
9. U.S. Health and Human Services Department, "Vaccine injury compensation table" *Health Resources and Services Administration,* http://www.hrsa.gov/vaccinecompensation/table.htm, accessed April 3, 2008.
10. K. Bohlke, R. Davis, S. Marcy, M. Braun, F. DeStefano, S. Black, J. Mullooly, and R. Thompson for the Vaccine Safety Datalink Team, "Risk of Anaphylaxis After Vaccination of Children and Adolescents," *Pediatrics* 112 (2003): 815–820.
11. M. Braun, G. Mootrey, M. Salive, R. Chen, S. Ellenberg, and the VAERS Working Group, "Infant immunization with acellular pertussis vaccines in the US: Assessment of the first two years' data from the Vaccine Adverse Event Reporting System (VAERS)," *Pediatrics* 106 (2000): e51.
12. L. Dillin, F. Hoaglund, and M. Scheck, "Brachial neuritis," *The Journal of Bone and Joint Surgery* 7 (1985): 878–880.
13. Centers for Disease Control and Prevention, "Mercury and Vaccines (Thimerosal)," http://www.cdc.gov/od/science/iso/concerns/thimerosal.htm accessed March 3, 2008.
14. Centers for Disease Control and Prevention, "History of Vaccine Safety," http://www.cdc.gov/od/science/iso/basic/history.htm, accessed March 31, 2008.
15. G. Gonçalves, M. Santos, J. Frade, and J. Cunha, "Levels of diphtheria and tetanus specific IgG of Portuguese adult women, before and after vaccination with adult type Td. Duration of immunity following vaccination," *BMC Public Health.* 7 (2007): 109–120.
16. R. Chen, I. Hardy, P. Rhodes, D. Tyshchenko, A. Moiseeva, and V. Marievsky, "Ukraine, 1992: First Assessment of Diphtheria Vaccine Effectiveness during the Recent Resurgence of Diphtheria in the Former Soviet Union," *The Journal of Infectious Diseases,* 181, Suppl 1 (2000): S178–183.
17. C. Vitek, "Diphtheria," *Current Topics in Microbiology and Immunology* 304 (2006): 71–94.

Chapter 6

1. Centers for Disease Control and Prevention, "Diphtheria Acquired by U.S. Citizens in the Russian Federation and Ukraine–1994," *Morbidity and Mortality Weekly Report* 44, 12 (1995): 237, 243–244.
2. S. Dittmann, M. Wharton, C. Vitek, M. Ciotti, A. Galazka, S. Guichard, I. Hardy,

U. Kartoglu, S. Koyama, J. Kreysler, B. Martin, D. Mercer, T. Rønne, C. Roure, R. Steinglass, P. Strebel, R. Sutter, and M. Trostle, "Successful Control of Epidemic Diphtheria in the States of the Former Union of Soviet Socialist Republics: Lessons Learned," *The Journal of Infectious Diseases* 181, Suppl 1 (2000): S10–22.

3. A. Galazkaa, "Implications of the Diphtheria Epidemic in the Former Soviet Union for Immunization Programs," *The Journal of Infectious Diseases* 181, Suppl 1 (2000): S244–248.

Chapter 7

1. K. McGinnis, M. Shapiro, J. Junkins-Hopkins, M. Smith, S. Lessin, C. Vittorio, and A. Rook, "Denileukin Diftitox for the Treatment of Panniculitic Lymphoma," *Archives of Dermatology* 138 (2002): 740–742.
2. B. Iglewski, and M. Rittenberg, "Selective Toxicity of Diphtheria Toxin for Malignant Cells," *Proc. Nat. Acad. Sci. USA* 71, 7 (1974): 2707–2710.
3. Y. Li, J. McCadden, F. Ferrer, M. Kruszewski, M. Carducci, J. Simons, and R. Rodriguez, "Prostate-specific Expression of the Diphtheria Toxin A Chain (DT-A): Studies of Inducibility and Specificity of Expression of Prostate-specific Antigen Promoter-driven DT-A Adenoviral-mediated Gene Transfer," *Cancer Research* 62 (2002): 2576–2582.
4. J. Edlund and T. Kuzel, "Denileukin diftitox: a concise clinical review," *Expert Reviews of Anticancer Therapies* 5, 1 (2005): 33–38.
5. ONTAK® (denileukin diftitox) package insert, Seragen, Incorporated, San Diego, Calif. http://www.fda.gov/cder/foi/label/2000/denser020599lb.pdf, accessed April 4, 2008.
6. A. Frankel, B. Powell, P. Hall, L. D. Case, and R. Kreitman, "Phase I Trial of a Novel Diphtheria Toxin/Granulocyte Macrophage Colony-stimulating Factor Fusion Protein (DT388GMCSF) for Refractory or Relapsed Acute Myeloid Leukemia," *Clinical Cancer Research* 8, (2002): 1004–1013.
7. J. Dannull, Z. Su, D. Rizzieri, B. Yang, D. Coleman, D. Yancey, A. Zhang, P. Dahm, N. Chao, E. Gilboa, and J. Vieweg, "Enhancement of vaccine-mediated antitumor immunity in cancer patients after depletion of regulatory T cells," *Journal of Clinical Investigation* 115 (2005): 3623–3633.
8. Y. Li, J. McCadden, F. Ferrer, M. Kruszewski, M. Carducci, J. Simons, and R. Rodriguez, "Prostate-specific Expression of the Diphtheria Toxin A Chain (DT-A): Studies of Inducibility and Specificity of Expression of Prostate-specific Antigen Promoter-driven DT-A Adenoviral-mediated Gene Transfer," *Cancer Research* 62 (2002): 2576–2582.
9. B. Brdar, M. Matuliæ, I. Rubelj, M. Ivankoviæ, E. Reichl, "Human Immunodeficiency Virus-1 tat- and tat/nef-defective Genomes Containing HIV-Regulated Diphtheria Toxin A Chain Gene Inhibit HIV Replication," *Croatian Medical Journal* 43, 5 (2002): 591–597.
10. V. Ho, D. Zahrieh, et. al., "Safety and efficacy of denileukin diftitox in patients with steroid-refractory acute graft versus host disease after allogenic hematopoietic stem cell transplantation," *Blood* 104 (2004): 1224–1226.
11. A. Martin, E. Gutierriz, J. Muglia, et al., "A multicenter dose-escalation trial with denileukin diftitox (Ontak, DAB(389) IL-2 in patients with severe psoriasis," *Journal of the American Academy of Dermatology* 45 (2001): 871–881.
12. C. Morin and R. Eckel, "Transgenic and knockout rodents: Novel insights into mechanisms of body weight regulation," *Journal of Nutritional Biochemistry* 8 (1997): 702–706.
13. J. Hansen and K. Kristiansen, "Regulatory circuits controlling white versus brown adipocyte differentiation," *Biochemical Journal* 398 (2006): 153–168.

Notes

Chapter 8

1. I. Mokrousov, O. Narvskaya, E. Limeschenko, and A. Vyazovaya, "Efficient Discrimination within a *Corynebacterium diphtheriae* Epidemic Clonal Group by a Novel Macroarray-Based Method," *Journal of Clinical Microbiology* 43, 4 (2005): 1662–1668.
2. Adapted from: Centers for Disease Control and Prevention, "CDC Health Information for International Travel 2008," http://wwwn.cdc.gov/travel/yellowBookCh4-Diphtheria.aspx, accessed March 31, 2008.
3. M. Rittenberg, C. T. Pinney Jr., and B. Iglewski, "Antigenic relationships on the diphtheria toxin molecule: antitoxin vs. antitoxoid," *Infection and Immunity* 14, 1 (1976): 122–128.
4. K. Lobeck, P. Drevet, M. Leonetti, C. Fromen-Romano, F. Ducancel, E. Lajeunesse, C. Lemaire, and A. Menez. "Towards a Recombinant Vaccine against Diphtheria Toxin," *Infection and Immunity* 66, 2 (1998): 418–423.
5. K. Killeen, V. Escuyer, J. Mekalanos, and R. Collier, "Reversion of recombinant toxoids: Mutations in diphtheria toxin that partially compensate for active-site deletions," *Microbiology* 89 (1992): 6207–6209.
6. B. Bissumbhar, A.G. Rakhmanova, G.A.M. Berbers, A. Iakolev, E. Nosikova, O. Melnick, E. Ovtcharenko, H.C. Rümke, and E.J. Ruitenberg, "Evaluation of diphtheria convalescent patients to serve as donors for the production of anti-diphtheria immunoglobulin preparations," *Vaccine* 22 (2004): 1886–1891.
7. J-H Cha, J. Brooke, M. Y. Chang, and L. Eidels, "Receptor-Based Antidote for Diphtheria," *Infection and Immunity* 70, 5 (2002): 2344–2350.
8. A. Cerdeno-Tarraga, A. Efstratioul, L. Dover, M. Holden, M. Pallen, S. Bentley, G. Besra, C. Churcher, K. James, A. De Zoysal, T. Chillingworth, A. Cronin, L. Dowd, T. Feltwell, N. Hamlin, S. Holroyd, K. Jagels, S. Moule, M. Quail, E. Rabbinowitsch, K. Rutherford, N. Thomson, L. Unwin, S. Whitehead, B. Barrell and J. Parkhill, "The complete genome sequence and analysis of *Corynebacterium diphtheriae* NCTC13129," *Nucleic Acids Research* 31, 22 (2003): 6516–6523.
9. S. Yellaboina, S. Ranjan, P. Chakhaiyar, S. Ehtesham Hasnain, and A. Ranjan, "Prediction of DtxR regulon: Identification of binding sites and operons controlled by diphtheria toxin repressor in *Corynebacterium diphtheriae*," *BMC Microbiology* 4 (2004): 38–45.
10. D. Marra Oram, A. Avdalovic, and R. Holmes, "Construction and Characterization of Transposon Insertion Mutations in *Corynebacterium diphtheriae* That Affect Expression of the Diphtheria Toxin Repressor (DtxR)," *Journal of Bacteriology* 184, 20 (2002): 5723–5732.

Glossary

adhesins—Bacterial proteins that allow binding to other cells.

adjuvant—A chemical that enhances the ability of a vaccine to induce an immune response. Currently, in the United States, alum (aluminum hydroxide) is the only approved adjuvant.

ADP ribosylation—A process where a chemical group (ADP-ribose) is added to another molecule, changing its activity. This is a common mechanism of action for many bacterial toxins. In the case of diphtheria toxin, the toxin adds ADP-ribose to a cellular protein called EF-2. The addition of ADP-ribose inactivates EF-2. As a consequence, the cell cannot make proteins, and it dies.

antibiotic resistance—A condition where bacteria are no longer killed or inhibited by an antibiotic. Antibiotic resistance results from a modification of the antibiotic target in the bacteria, from inactivation of the antibiotic by the microbe, or from other causes.

antibiotics—Chemicals, produced by bacteria or fungi, that kill or inhibit the growth of bacteria without harming the human host.

antibodies—Protein molecules, made by cells of the immune system, that attack foreign materials in the body, such as toxins.

antitoxin—A medical treatment for diseases caused by toxins. The antitoxin consists of antibodies, proteins made in an animal, that attach to and inactivate toxins.

assay—A procedure or technique for detecting a substance. In the context used in this book, an assay is a procedure or technique for detecting a specific bacterium, *C. diphtheriae*, or diphtheria toxin.

attenuate—A treatment that reduces or eliminates the potency of a toxin or virulence of a pathogen. For example, the diphtheria toxin was attenuated by treatment with formaldehyde to allow it to be used in a vaccine.

avirulent—Unable to cause disease. Usually refers to a strain of normally pathogenic bacteria that has been rendered noninfectious as the result of a mutation.

bacterial virus—Also known as a bacteriophage. A virus that infects bacterial cells; often only a specific strain or species of bacteria can be infected by a specific virus.

base pair—A common measure of DNA size—a base pair is the smallest information unit in DNA. Chemically, a base pair involves two subunits of

DNA (nucleotides) that are on opposite strands of DNA and that interact with one another.

biotypes—Distinct populations within a bacterial species that have some unique characteristics, such as greater or lesser virulence.

blood serum—The components of the blood with the blood cells removed. Serum contains antibodies, which are used as a treatment for some diseases, including diphtheria.

Corynebacterium diphtheriae—The bacterium that causes diphtheria.

cytoplasm—The primary constituent of a cell, located inside the cellular membrane.

diphthamide—A modified histidine amino acid that is the target for diphtheria toxin.

diphtheria—An acute infectious disease, usually characterized by inflammation of the throat, the presence of a pseudomembrane, and the production of a toxin that can damage the throat and other tissues.

***dtx*R**—A gene in *Corynebacterium diphtheriae* that regulates the production of toxin. If iron levels in the cell are high, the DtxR protein is active and binds to a site on the DNA near the toxin gene, preventing the toxin from being produced. If iron levels in the cell are low, the DtxR protein is inactive, it cannot bind to DNA, and diphtheria toxin is produced.

elongation factor-2 (EF-2)—The component of the cell that is inactivated by diphtheria toxin. Normally, elongation factor-2 helps the cell make proteins. Diphtheria inactivates this factor by adding a chemical group to it (ADP-Ribose). As a result, the cell is unable to make proteins, and the cell dies.

endemic—(Of a disease) Continually present in a country or region.

enzyme—A protein catalyst. Catalysts are molecules that can repeatedly carry out a chemical reaction without being used up in the process.

enzyme immunoassay—A technique for identifying a bacterium using antibodies containing an identifying molecule. If the bacterium is present, the antibodies will bind to it and the identifying molecule (typically an enzyme) carried by the antibodies can be detected.

fimbriae—Small hairlike projections on the surface of bacterial cells that are often involved in the attachment of the bacteria to human cells.

gram positive—A term used to describe certain types of bacteria, including the microbe that causes diphtheria. Gram-positive bacteria have a thick cell wall and a single cell membrane; as a consequence they stain purple when stained with a set of dyes. This purple color is considered gram positive (as compared with gram-negative bacteria, which stain pink).

intubation—A medical procedure where a plastic tube is inserted down a patient's throat into the trachea to prevent suffocation. It is sometimes used in cases of diphtheria to prevent suffocation if a patient's pseudomembrane completely blocks the throat.

leukemia—A group of cancers that involve white blood cells.

lymph nodes—Small nodules containing immune system cells that filter bacteria and other foreign particles from fluid from the tissues (lymphatic fluid).

lymphoma—Cancer of the lymph nodes.

mobile genetic elements—A section of DNA that contains functions that allows it to insert into various locations in the genome of an organism.

polymerase chain reaction (PCR)—A technique used to amplify short DNA sequences. In the clinical laboratory, this technique is sometimes used to identify *C. diphtheriae.*

pseudomembrane—A flap of tissue found in the throat of individuals with diphtheria. This membrane results from the action of the bacterial toxin and consists of the remains of dead cells, bacteria, and other debris.

pure culture—A preparation that contains only a single species of bacteria.

receptor-mediated endocytosis—A process for bringing materials into cells that cannot pass directly across a membrane. Substances bind to a receptor protein on the surface of the membrane; this binding triggers the cell to engulf the receptor and the substance bound to the receptor. This process is exploited by diphtheria toxin for entry into human cells.

recombinant DNA—Laboratory-manipulated DNA. In many cases, DNA from two different organisms is combined, thus producing recombinant DNA. An example is the combination of the DNA for the diphtheria toxin from *C. diphtheria* being placed together with the DNA from the human IL-2 gene to produce the anticancer drug denileukin diftitox.

Schick test—A method for determining if a person is susceptible to diphtheria. A small amount of diphtheria toxin is injected under the skin. If a person is susceptible to the disease, they develop a reddish welt at the site of the injection.

sterile—Without any living organisms.

toxoid—An inactivated toxin that is used in several vaccines, including the vaccine for diphtheria.

tracheotomy—A surgical method for creating an opening in the front of the neck to allow a tube to be placed through the skin into the trachea (windpipe). It is one method used to prevent suffocation in diphtheria patients whose throats are blocked with a pseudomembrane.

virulence factors—Molecules or processes that enhance the ability of a pathogen to cause disease. For example, in diphtheria, the toxin is the primary virulence factor, as strains of *C. diphtheriae* lacking the toxin gene do not produce diphtheria.

Further Resources

Hammonds, Evelynn Maxine. *Childhood's Deadly Scourge: The Campaign to Control Diphtheria in New York City, 1880–1930.* Baltimore: Johns Hopkins University Press, 2002.

Linton, Derek S. *Emil Von Behring: Infectious Disease, Immunology, Serum Therapy.* Philadelphia: American Philosophical Society, 2005.

Salisbury, Gay, and Laney Salisbury. *The Cruelest Miles: The Heroic Story of Dogs and Men in a Race Against an Epidemic.* New York: W.W. Norton & Co., 2003.

Silverstein, Arthur M., and Paul Ehrlich. *Paul Ehrlich's Receptor Immunology: The Magnificent Obsession.* San Diego: Academic Press, 2002.

Wharton, Melinda. "Control of Epidemic Diphtheria in the Newly Independent States of the Former Soviet Union, 1990–1998." *Journal of Infectious Diseases,* v. 181, suppl. 1. Chicago: University of Chicago Press, 2000.

Wheeler, Ben S. *Trends in Diphtheria Research.* New York: Nova Science Publishers, 2006.

Web Sites

Centers for Disease Control and Prevention, Diphtheria.
http://www.cdc.gov/ncidod/dbmd/diseaseinfo/Diphtheria_t.htm

Mayo Clinic, Diphtheria
http://www.mayoclinic.com/health/diphtheria/DS00495

Medline Plus, Diphtheria
http://www.nlm.nih.gov/medlineplus/ency/article/001608.htm

K. Todar's Online Textbook of Bacteriology
http://www.textbookofbacteriology.net/diphtheria.html

Index

Index

About the Author

Patrick Guilfoile earned his Ph.D. in bacteriology at the University of Wisconsin–Madison. He subsequently did postdoctoral research at that institution, as well as at the Whitehead Institute for Biomedical Research at the Massachusetts Institute of Technology. He is a professor of biology at Bemidji State University in northern Minnesota. Currently on leave from his faculty position, he is presently an associate dean at the university. His most recent research has focused on the molecular genetics of ticks and other parasites. He has authored or coauthored more than 20 papers in scientific and biology education journals. He has also written two other books in this series, along with a molecular biology laboratory manual and a book on controlling ticks that transmit Lyme disease.

About the Consulting Editor

Hilary Babcock, M.D., M.P.H., is an assistant professor of medicine at Washington University School of Medicine and the medical director of occupational health for Barnes–Jewish Hospital and St. Louis Children's Hospital. She received her undergraduate degree from Brown University and her M.D. from the University of Texas Southwestern Medical Center at Dallas. After completing her residency, chief residency, and infectious disease fellowship at Barnes–Jewish Hospital, she joined the faculty of the infectious disease division. She completed an M.P.H. in Public Health from St. Louis University School of public health in 2006. She has lectured, taught, and written extensively about infectious diseases, their treatment, and their prevention. She is a member of numerous medical associations and is board certified in infectious disease. She lives in St. Louis, Missouri.